Free Verse Editions

Edited by Jon Thompson

AN UNCHANGING BLUE

SELECTED POEMS 1962-1975

Rolf Dieter Brinkmann

Translated by Mark Terrill

Parlor Press
Anderson, South Carolina
www.parlorpress.com

Parlor Press LLC, West Lafayette, Indiana 47906

Printed in the United States of America
S A N: 2 5 4 - 8 8 7 9

Library of Congress Cataloging-in-Publication Data

Brinkmann, Rolf Dieter.
An unchanging blue : selected poems 1962-1975 / Rolf Dieter Brinkmann ; translated by Mark Terrill.
p. cm. -- (Free verse editions)
ISBN 978-1-60235-198-1 (pbk. : acid-free paper) -- ISBN 978-1-60235-199-8 (adobe ebook)
1. Brinkmann, Rolf Dieter--Translations into English. I. Terrill, Mark. II. Title.
PT2662.R52A2 2011
831'.914--dc23

2011025011

Cover design by David Blakesley.
Cover Images: "Collage" by Rolf Dieter Brinkmann and "Rolf Dieter Brinkmann with Super 8 camera, Cologne, Hohe Straße, July 1968." © 1968 by Jens Hagen" Used by permission.

Printed on acid-free paper.

Parlor Press, LLC is an independent publisher of scholarly and trade titles in print and multimedia formats. This book is available in paperback from Parlor Press on the World Wide Web at http://www.parlorpress.com or through online and brick-and-mortar bookstores. For submission information or to find out about Parlor Press publications, write to Parlor Press, 3015 Brackenberry Drive, Anderson, South Carolina, 29621, or e-mail editor@parlorpress.com.

Contents

From *Die Piloten* (1968)

From *Standphotos* (1969)

From *Gras* (1970)

From *Westwärts 1 & 2* (1975)

Introduction

Rolf Dieter Brinkmann was born in Vechta, Germany, on April 16th, 1940, in the midst of World War II, and died on April 23rd, 1975, in London, England, after being struck by a hit-and-run driver while crossing the street to enter a pub. Brinkmann had been in London after being invited to read at the Cambridge Poetry Festival, where he read with John Ashbery, Ed Dorn, Lee Harwood and others. In May, 1975, just a few weeks after his death, Brinkmann's seminal, parameter-expanding poetry collection *Westwärts 1 & 2* appeared, which was posthumously awarded the prestigious Petrarca Prize.

Brinkmann grew up in the predominantly catholic, conservative atmosphere of provincial Northern Germany during the Adenauer era. His father worked as a civil servant; his mother died of cancer in 1957. In 1958, already a difficult and critical student, Brinkmann was forced to leave school after organizing a presentation with lectures about Sartre and existentialism, the lyrical work of Benn and Brecht, as well as the writing of Pound, Rimbaud, Stramm, Hesse, and Heinrich Heine; all apparently too radical for the post-war German school regime. During this time Brinkmann made his first serious attempts at writing poetry, mostly in the tradition of European modernism. In 1958, after having left school, Brinkmann made a trip through Belgium and on to Paris. In 1959 he began an apprenticeship as a book-seller in Essen, Germany, where he also met his later friend and collaborator, Ralf Rainer Rygulla, who was to play an important role in Brinkmann's life as a writer.

In 1960 Brinkmann published his first poems, and in 1961, he moved to Cologne and began studying at the Pädagogische Hochschule. In 1964 he married Maleen Brinkmann, and their son, Robert, was born, who suffered severe brain damage during his birth. In Cologne, Brinkmann met Dieter Wellershof, who at the time worked as an editor at the Kiepenhauer & Witsch Verlag, a distinguished and well known publishing house. Also at this time, Brinkmann received a prize for young artists from the state of Nordrhein-Westfalen. Beginning in 1965, he undertook a series of visits to London, in part to visit his friend, Ralf Rainer Rygulla. In 1968

Brinkmann began experimenting with 8mm film and made several multi-media presentations of his work. At the University of Cologne Brinkmann organized a teach-in which directed criticism towards various aspects of contemporary popular culture, thus estranging himself from the politically engaged student movement. Also at this time, Brinkmann was commissioned by WDR (West German Television) to write a script about the rise and fall of a rock star, called *Der Abstieg* (The Fall). During a public discussion at the Academy of Art in West Berlin with the critics Rudolf Hartung and Marcel Reich-Ranicki, Brinkmann turned the occasion into a minor scandal ("If this book was a machine gun, I'd shoot you with it. ")

In 1969 Brinkmann joined up with Dieter Wellershof, Peter Handke and several other writers to produce a small-press literary magazine entitled *Gummibaum* (*Rubber Tree*), which was printed in small editions and distributed in and around Cologne. In 1970 he began to experiment with photography, a medium which became increasingly present in his work. From 1972 to 1973 he was an artist-in-residence at the Deutsche Akadamie Villa Massimo in Rome. During this time Brinkmann went into a self-imposed exile, distancing himself completely from his friends and colleagues, and turning against the politically engaged literature of the sixties, as well as his own contributions to Pop literature, eventually isolating himself from the German literary scene altogether. In 1974 Brinkmann was a visiting writer at the Department of German at the University of Austin in Texas. In April, 1975, Brinkmann went to England to take part in the Cambridge Poetry Festival, and where he met his untimely and tragic death in the streets of London. His remains were shipped back to Germany and he was buried in the family plot of the cemetery in Vechta.

Considered to be one of the most important poets of post-war Germany, Brinkmann's work is definitely in the marginal outsider vein, approximating a sort of German hybrid of Frank O'Hara, William Burroughs, and W.C. Williams, all of whom were important influences on Brinkmann's work. His permanent confrontation with the post-war German literary establishment (reminding one at times of Jack Spicer and his place in American poetry), and his envelope-pushing experiments with language, syntax and semantics (taken to the extreme in *Westwärts 1 & 2*), led him further and further away from the literary scene. His confrontational nature and volatile personality were feared at readings, and together with his huge creative output and his early death, earned him a reputation as the "James Dean of poetry," a true enfant terrible of contemporary letters. Contrary to his public image, he was known among his friends and colleagues as warm and generous, with a sparkling and spontaneous sense of humor.

During his lifetime, Brinkmann published nine poetry collections, four short story collections, several radio plays, and a highly acclaimed novel, *Keiner weiß mehr* (*No One Knows More*). He also edited and translated two German-language anthologies of contemporary American poetry (primarily Beat and New York School, for which Brinkmann had a particular affinity), and translated Frank O'Hara's *Lunch Poems* into German, as well as a collection of Ted Berrigan, entitled *Guillaume Apollinaire ist Tot*. During the last years of his life, Brinkmann devoted much of his time to collecting audio, film and photo material, as well as copious notes, for a planned multi-media novel which remained uncompleted at the time of his death. Since Brinkmann's death, several of his journals have appeared in print, all employing a montage/cut-up technique somewhat reminiscent of Burroughs, and displaying a remorseless self-scrutiny and microscopic attention to details, as well as an eye-catching sense for graphics. A feature-length film directed by Harald Bergmann, entitled *Brinkmann's Wrath*, was recently produced in Germany, and a new expanded edition of *Westwärts 1 & 2* appeared in 2005, which marked the 30th anniversary of Brinkmann's death.

My previous collection of Brinkmann translations, *Like a Pilot* (Sulphur River Literary Review Press, Austin, 2001), was made up of a selection of poems taken from *Standphotos* (Rowohlt Verlag, Hamburg, 1980), which incorporates the nine volumes of poetry published during Brinkmann's lifetime. My criterion for choosing the poems that made up that collection was that they be the most representative of what Brinkmann had achieved *prior* to the publication of *Westwärts 1 & 2*. A man and a woman in a bleak apartment in an even bleaker metropolis, ostensibly discussing some inanimate object, the conversation a rhetorical Ping-Pong game symbolizing some greater urgency, some potential crisis, an underlying decay of the existential status quo; this was typical Brinkmann country. "Personism" and postmodernism in a high-speed collision on the German autobahn. The frequency of appearances by various Pop icons, be they Godzilla, Batman, Humphrey Bogart, or Ava Gardner's toe, was roughly in real-time, and not an intentional amplification on my part; many of Brinkmann's poems deal with contemporary Pop culture again and again, a curious phenomena considering the circumstances of his life, i.e., being born in the midst of World War II in Germany.

Rarely if at all does Brinkmann deal with the various hardships and depravations that he must have experienced as a child in wartime and post-war Germany. Rather than being obsessed with the question of collective guilt that so preoccupied other post-war German writers, Brinkmann's stance was one of absolute immediacy; forever looking at the world in the here-and-now, without a trace of sentimentality or nostalgia. When not deconstructing contemporary culture and employing his sardonic wit, Brinkmann could be frighteningly stark and photographically precise, both in the use of his language and the graphic representation of his images. Brinkmann was forever experimenting, constantly morphing from one creative incarnation to the next, and was a definite forerunner of postmodernism, from his earliest attempts at quasi-traditional European modernism up to his final broken-stanza, irregular-enjambment explorations incorporating his relentless questioning of everyday existence and his gift for saying so much with so little, no small feat in the German language.

Brinkmann's sudden and accidental death came as a surprise to all. He had frequently alluded to death in his writing, and often mentioned his fears of cancer or even an accidental death in his letters. When an artist such as Brinkmann, at the peak of his powers, constantly morphing from one creative incarnation to the next, is suddenly removed from this life—intentionally or unintentionally—it is nothing other than a major tragedy and a great loss. Thirty-five years after his death, it's both difficult and painful to speculate as to what Rolf Dieter Brinkmann might have gone on to achieve. Already the poems in *Westwärts 1 & 2* represent a quantum leap from the work in *Standphotos.* His sprawling, all-over-the-page poems all seem to start where Frank O'Hara's "Biotherm" and Ted Berrigan's "Tambourine Life" left off. And in *Westwärts 1 & 2* we find a most decisively political poet indeed, the title poem taking on the rise and fall of Western civilization and culture, while simultaneously tracing the inherent damage incurred by the psyche (both collective and individual), in series after series of multi-lingual, modular stanzas that can be read in whatever order the reader chooses. *Westwärts 1 & 2* represents not only the culmination of Brinkmann's career as a poet, but also stands as a milestone in modern European poetry, much of it seeming almost more relevant today than when it appeared thirty-five years ago. It also shows the amazing developments he made as a poet in the five-year interim since the publication of his previous collection, *Gras*, in 1970. The influence of the New American Poetry and especially the New York School (both generations) make *Westwärts 1 & 2* even more interesting and accessible to American readers, providing a sort of reverse-angle perspective on one of the liveliest epochs in American poetry. *Westwärts 1 & 2* is a highly significant work that bridges two cultures via aesthetically daring, critical and irreverent poetics, and definitely warrants a much wider audience.

The final poem in this collection, "Some Very Popular Songs," is one of several longer poems in *Westwärts 1 & 2*. The poem moves forward and backward through time and space, and shows clearly how Brinkmann was becoming more and more political in the course of his development as a writer. Presenting Adolf Hitler as a human being, with his love affair with Eva Braun, was a very radical move for a German writer in the politically turbulent seventies in West Germany. "Some Very Popular Songs" incorporates many of Brinkmann's signature traits; social/political criticism, intense self-scrutiny, taboo-breaking, travel diaries reworked as poetry, and his trademark trenchant humor.

—*Mark Terrill*

1

An Unchanging Blue

2

Zwischenzeiten

Hand vor Augen oder Hand nicht
vor Augen denn das Licht
wechselt vom Wasser
zum Baum: da
ist es ein Vogel oder nicht ein Vogel
ein Elephant
eine Schnecke
in Abständen
betrachtet vom Balkon aus
doch war kein Balkon
dann vom Fenster her aber nicht
vom Fenster in der Tür stehend
die Hand vor Augen als es
vorbeikam
nicht eintrat
fortging
während die Schatten
wechselten von einer Stimme
zur anderen war
es Fisch war
es Vogel
gewiß nicht noch war es hell nicht
Tag mehr auch nicht Nacht zu dieser
Zeit

Between-Times

Hand before the eyes or hand not
before the eyes then the light
changes from the water
to the tree: there
is it a bird or not a bird
an elephant
a snail
in intervals
observed from a balcony
no not a balcony
then from a window but not
from a window standing in the door
the hand before the eyes as it
came by
did not come in
went away
while the shadows
changed from one mood
to another was
it a fish
a bird
certainly not it was still light no
longer day not night either at this
time

Von der Gegenständlichkeit eines Gedichtes

Die Farbe
der Tinte ist königsblau
die Feder aus Stahl
schreibt die Worte
auf das weiße Papier

die angewandte Grammatik enthält
nichts über Wetteraussichten
und sie mißt dem
Vogelflug nicht die geheime Formel bei
leichter zu sein als die Schwermut ohne Regel
ist die Landschaft angeordnet
das Blattgrün ist fehlerlos die
Bäume verbergen der
vorhanden Sprache
die innere Wildnis

mit der Feder
aus Stahl schreibe ich
die Worte auf das weiße
Papier die Farbe
der Tinte ist
königsblau

Of the Representativeness of a Poem

The color
of the ink is royal blue
the steel pen nib
writes the words
on the white paper

the applied grammar contains
nothing about the weather forecast
and it does not measure the
flight of the bird against the secret formula of
being lighter than the melancholy without rules
is the landscape in order
the leaf-green is faultless the
trees hide the
available language
of the internal wilderness

with the pen nib
of steel I write
the words on the white
paper the color
of the ink is
royal blue

Das Schweigen

Das Schweigen
schwärzt die Stimme an sie
reden weiter mit dem
Bauch die Worte
steigen himmelan es
grünt die Zunge
es sprengt
der Zahn die Stimme
schwärzt die Sprache an sie
drehen ihre
Kehlen um es
kräht im Hof dreimal
der Hahn die
Lunge platzt
von Asthma
frei die Sprache
schwärzt die Leute an die
haben keine Stimmen
mehr der Mund
ist leer das
Ohr vernahm
ein Schweigen

The Silence

The silence
blackens the voice they
continue talking with the
stomach the words
climb skyward it
turns the tongue green
it explodes
the tooth the voice
blackens the language they
turn their
throats around
the cock in the courtyard
crows three times the
lungs burst
from asthma
the language free
blackens the people they
have no more voices
the mouth
is empty the
ear heard
a silence

Die Stimmen

Die Stimmen stehen
zu lange am Kai Schiffe siehst du nicht mehr
unter den Bäumen wir wollen dort
fortfahren in Überhäufung ich war
das will ich sagen
nie in Amsterdam sah in
einem Bild sie stehen
standen zu lange
im Herbst noch draußen vergessen im Schatten
hielten dort an den Grachten übers Brückengeländer
gelehnt die Stimmen
standen hielten Laub
für Worte
wollten nicht Vögel sein
wovon ich mehr
berichten
will sie standen an den Kais zu lange
waren sich einig
fegten die Straßen
gingen auch stolz Dachrinnen entlang
gefielen sich selber
in Fenstern beim Flüstern
oder im Wasser
doch war ich nie in Amsterdam
auch Schiffe siehst du nicht mehr
viel zu dieser Jahreszeit

The Voices

The voices stand
too long on the quay you don't see ships anymore
under the trees we want to go there
to keep on heaping up I was
I want to say
never in Amsterdam saw
them in a picture standing
stood too long
in the autumn still outside forgotten in the shadows
stopped there along the canals above the bridge railings
the voices leaned,
stood, took leaves
for words
did not want to be birds
about which I want to
say more
they stood on the quays too long
were united
swept the streets
went proudly along the rain gutters
liked themselves
in windows with whispering
or in the water
but I was never in Amsterdam
and ships you don't see much
anymore this time of year

Heute

Der
kleine Himmel heute, der
sehr schnell vergeht
(zwischen zwei
Uhren, in denen
der Tod wohnt)
findet sich wieder
auf der Leinwand Rousseaus
oder nach Jahren in einem
fremden Gedicht: da
stehen wir
sprachlos
am Fenster
und begreifen nicht
mehr, wie es verschwand
(zwischen zwei
Uhren, in denen
der Tod wohnt).

Today

The
small sky today, which
passes very quickly
(between two
clocks in which
Death lives)
finds itself again
on a canvas from Rousseau
or years later in a
strange poem: there
we stand
speechless
at the window
and no longer under-
stand, how it disappeared
(between two
clocks in which
Death lives).

Verwechslung

In dem kleinen
Obstladen der Seitenstraße
kurz nach Ladenschluß, sagte sie.
Zur gleichen Zeit
überquert ein Mann
die Kreuzung.
Obstläden solcher
Art gibts viele.

Confusion

In the little
fruit market in the side street
just after closing, she said.
At the very same time
a man crossed
the intersection.
Such fruit markets
are everywhere.

Immer mehr Worte

Immer mehr
Worte wachsen über
Nacht der schwarzen Farbe
zu, die ihr Meer
zwischen uns
treibt, darin
wir nicht
ablassen
von der entsetzlichen
Mühsal zu lieben

wenn ich
Matrose wär
oder ein Hund mit
einem Anker tätowiert
auf der Stirn, ich
würd hoch auf
dem Meer nach
deinem Mund
suchen

dann
müßte die Sprache leicht
sein wie der Tod
und so schnell: es
gibt zuvieles
was ich nicht
sagen kann.

Always More Words

Always more
words growing over-
night into the blackness
whose ocean
roils between us
in which we
won't let go
of the dreadful
effort to love

if I
was a sailor
or a dog with
an anchor tattooed
on my forehead, I
would sail
far out to sea
searching for
your mouth

then
the language must be
light as death
and just as fast:
there is so much
which I can
not say.

Heimliche Souvenirs

Der Haken
der sich langsam krümmt
oder die Rasierklinge
die Rasierklinge
die ansetzt

am Handgelenk
und eine kleine Wunde hinterläßt
die Zange, die reißt an den Augen
die stählerne Zange

die Feder
die zittert im Nacken
Wülste, rosafarbene Narben
und erste, stille Blutung

und das Bild
das Bild von der Kommunion
der lange, verknitterte Anzug
das Ohr von van Gogh

aufbewahrt
in einem kleinen
mit roter Seide ausgeschlagenen
Kasten unter dem Bett.

Secret Souvenirs

The hook
which slowly bends
or the razorblade
the razorblade
that touches

at the wrist
and leaves behind a small wound
the pliers, they tear at the eyes
the steel pliers

the feather
it quivers at the bulging
neck, pink-colored scars
and an initial, silent bleeding

and the picture
the picture from the communion
the long, wrinkled suit
the ear of van Gogh

saved
in a small
red silk-lined
box under the bed.

Schnee

Schnee: wer
dieses Wort zu Ende
denken könnte
bis dahin
wo es sich auflöst
und wieder zu Wasser wird

das die Wege aufweicht
und den Himmel in
einer schwarzen

blanken Pfütze
spiegelt, als wär er
aus nichtrostendem Stahl

und bliebe
unverändert blau.

Snow

Snow: who
could think this word
through to the end
to there
where it dissolves
and becomes water again

that softens the paths
and reflects the sky
in a dark

shiny puddle,
as though it were
made of stainless steel

and would remain
an unchanging blue.

Auf einem falschen Ast

Er sitzt
auf einem falschen Ast
und singt.

Die Leute
die vorübergehen
sagen: er sitzt auf einem
falschen Ast
und singt
und singt.

Tatsache ist
und allen bekannt
er sitzt auf einem falschen Ast
und singt
und singt

und singt
auf einem falschen Ast
mitten im März
allein.

On a Mistaken Branch

He sits
on a mistaken branch
and sings.

The people
who pass by
say: he sits on a
mistaken branch
and sings
and sings.

Fact is
and known to all
he sits on a mistaken branch
and sings
and sings

and sings
on a mistaken branch
in the middle of March
alone.

Gedichte schreiben

O, die alltäglichen Dinge
die alltäglichen Dinge

der Postbote
frühmorgens

wirft Rechnungen
und Drucksachen

Briefe und
Postkarten

ins Haus—
er glaubt nicht

an Gedichte
und Stilleben

an Regen
und Schnee

als poetisches
Bild

und nutzt die Schuhsohlen ab
und schleppt an der Tasche—

er würde
viel lieber

den Garten umgraben
ein paar Beete anlegen

ein Bier trinken
im Schatten dann liegen

die Briefe vergessen
die Türen vergessen

und all die Dinge
und all die Dinge.

Writing Poems

O, the everyday things
the everyday things

the mailman
early mornings

stuffs bills
and flyers

letters and
postcards

into the house—
he doesn't believe

in poems
and still lifes

in rain
and snow

as poetic
image

and wears down his soles
and lugs his mail bag—

he would
much rather

dig in the garden
plant a few flowers

drink a beer
and lie in the shade

forgetting the letters
forgetting the doors

and all these things
and all these things.

Was soll das

Noten
Himmelsschlüssel
das erste Blatt einer Geranie
die schon totgeglaubt
und fortgeworfen
war—

was soll das?
Besser als ein Gedicht
ist eine Tür, die
schließt.

What's the Purpose

Notes
primrose
the first leaf of a geranium
already assumed dead
and thrown
away—

what's the purpose?
Better than a poem
is a door, that
shuts.

Gedicht am 19. März 1964

Ein Bleistift
ein Blatt Papier
eine Tasse Kaffee
eine Zigarette

der letzte Schlager
der Rolling Stones
der kommende Frühling
das Familienbild

eine Hand
einige Worte
ein Auge
ein Mund.

Poem on March 19th, 1964

A pencil
a sheet of paper
a cup of coffee
a cigarette

the latest hit
from the Rolling Stones
the approaching spring
the family portrait

a hand
a few words
an eye
a mouth.

Schlaf

Schlaf
schwarze Zone, die
auf dem Grund
der Membrane
liegt

wie Wind
der weder Türen
noch Fenster
kennt

aber
einmal
da öffnet sich ein Leib
der keiner ist
und wirft
einen Schatten

einmal
gibt es Schatten, die
nie von lebendigen
Körpern getragen
wurden

die Schatten
von Hunden, abgemagert
bis auf Kopf
und Füße

Hunde
die als Wörter
durch die Hände
rinnen

Wörter, die
rosa Tiere aus Plastik.

Sleep

Sleep
black zone, which
lies at the
bottom
of the membrane

like wind
that knows neither
doors nor
windows

but
one time
a body that it is not
a body opens itself
and casts
a shadow

one time
there are shadows which
are never worn
by living
bodies

the shadows
of dogs, skin and bones
but for their heads
and feet

dogs
which run
through the hands
as words

words, the
pink plastic animals.

Einfache Gedanken über meinen Tod

Er
wird kommen, weder
mit einem Messer
in der Hand
noch mit
Gebrüll

er wird kommen
wie einer, der zufällig
vorübergeht und nach der Uhrzeit fragt
er wird kommen und seinen Hut lüften

elfter Februar
Neunzehnhundertdreiundsechzig, kurz
nach elf Uhr, der Morgen
ohne besondere
Aussicht, wenig
Licht, das
hereinfällt
in mein Zimmer, Engelbertstraße
vierter Stock

und er wird kommen
er wird den Strom ablesen
und das Gas

er wird
die Tür schließen, höflich
wie jemand, der sich
nicht auskennt
im Leben.

Simple Thoughts About my Death

He
will come, neither
with a knife
in his hand
nor with
a roar

he will come
like someone who happens
to pass by and asks about the time
he will come and tip his hat

February eleventh
nineteenhundredandsixtythree, just
past eleven, the morning
with no special
perspectives, very
little light
falling into
my room, Engelbertstraße
fourth floor

and he will come
and read the electricity
and gas meters

he will
shut the door, politely
like someone who
doesn't know his way
around in life.

10 Uhr 20

Die Frau
tritt aus dem Haus
und leert den Eimer, ehe
sie in die Stadt geht.
Überall ist
das Licht.
Langsam überquert
ein Krüppel die Straße.
Überall stehen
die Fenster
voll Licht.
Aus der Wohnung
nebenan kommt
Klaviermusik.

20 Past 10

The woman
steps out of the house
and empties the pail, before
she goes into the city.
Everywhere is
that light.
Slowly a cripple
crosses the street.
Everywhere the
windows are
full of light.
From the apartment
next door comes
piano music.

Dieses Zimmer

Dieses Zimmer
ist viel zu eng
zum Atmen, darin ich untergeh
in rotem Plüsch, du fragst
nach mir, wer ich
denn sei, ich
bin uralt, die
Antwort stimmt
genau, ich sitze tief
im Plüsch, ich atme
Staub, siehst du
ich bin die
Stimme tief
im Plüsch, ich
atme tief, und wenn
du fragst, wer ich denn sei
ich bin die Fliege an der Wand, die
langsam sinkt, ich bin die Uhr, die
läuft zurück in diesem
Zimmer, viel zu eng
in dieser Gruft
aus rotem
Plüsch, und fragst
du noch, wer sitzt im Plüsch
ruf ich nach dir aus rotem
Plüsch, aus rotem
Stoff, ich bin
der Stoff
uralt der
Stoff, die
Antwort stimmt, genau.

This Room

This room
is much too cramped
to breathe in, in which I drown
in red plush, you ask
about me, who I
am, I am
ancient, the
answer is correct,
exact, I sit deep
in the plush, I breathe
dust, you see
I am the
voice deep
in the plush, I
breathe deep, and when
you ask, then who am I,
I'm the fly on the wall, which
slowly sinks, I'm the clock, which
runs backwards in this
room, much too cramped
in this crypt
of red
plush, and should you
ask again, who sits in the plush
I call after you out of red
plush, out of red
material, I am
the material
ancient the
material, the
answer correct, exact.

Hölderlin-Herbst

Auf
den Baustellen
wird jetzt Tag
und Nacht gearbeitet.
Auch die Gärten
werden nicht
geschont.
Sie werden
mit rostigen Harken
durchkämmt nach den
letzten Möhren
und Kartoffeln.
(Der Grünkohl
darf stehenbleiben
bis der erste Frost
gekommen ist.)
Weiter draußen
schlachten sie Schweine.
Frisch gewaschen und gebürstet
hängen die offenen Leiber
weiß an den Leitern.

Hölderlin-Autumn

At
the construction sites
the work goes on
night and day.
Even the gardens
are not
spared.
They're combed
with rusty rakes
looking for the
last carrots
and potatoes.
(The kale
is allowed
to stay until
the first frost.)
Further out
they're slaughtering pigs.
Freshly washed and scrubbed
the opened bodies hang
white on the ladders.

Wechselt die Jahreszeit

Die
straffen Brüste
siebzehnjähriger
pullovertragender
Mädchen sind
schöner im
Regen, wie
sie versteckt
unter den leichten
Nylonmänteln hüpfen
beim Überspringen
von Pfützen auf dem
Bürgersteig: Wer denkt
dann noch an
gewagte Metaphern
angesichts so vieler
Ausdrucksmöglichkeiten
für einunddasselbe
Bild?

Noch
ehe der Nachmittag
vergeht vor lauter
Regenschirmen, hohen
Schuhen und
Südwestern
wechselt die
Jahreszeit.

Change of Seasons

The
firm breasts of
seventeen-year-old
pullover-wearing
girls are more
beautiful in
the rain, the way
they hop
hidden under the
light nylon jackets
while jumping over
the puddles on the
sidewalk. Who still
thinks about
daring metaphors
in the face of so many
possibilities of expression
for one and the same
picture?

And
before the afternoon
disappears in
umbrellas, high
shoes and
sou'westers
the season
is changing.

Gedicht vor Anfang des Winters

Die Sätze
werden langsam wieder
schwerer. Es liegt
vielleicht an
der Luft, oder
daß ich nicht
fortgezogen bin
zur rechten Zeit?

Die Luft
ist die gleiche
wie gestern. Gestern
lag ein Steinschlag
darin, heute erst
trifft das
Geröll, das
Überflüssige, der Schrei
ein wirres Sprechen
von Händen und
Fingern.

Das geht
schnell vorbei. Schneller
als ich gedacht habe. Gleich
ist es Winter, und die
Cafés sind alle
geschlossen.

Poem Before the Beginning of Winter

The sentences
are slowly becoming heavier
again. Maybe it's
something in
the air, or
that I haven't
gone away
at the right time?

The air
is the same
as yesterday. Yesterday
it was full of
falling rocks
only today
do the boulders arrive,
the superfluous, the scream
of a confused speech
of hands and
fingers.

That goes
by quickly. Faster
than I thought. Straightaway
it's winter, and the
cafés are all
closed.

Ein einziger Satz

oder gleich
mehrere. Hintereinander.
Ein ganzes Blumenbeet.

Und wieder Sätze.
Andere. Andere
Blumen, ein für alle Mal.
Endgültig.

Blumen, die
Wurzeln treiben—
zu fragen bliebe
wofür.

A Single Sentence

or even
several. One after the other.
An entire flower bed.

And again sentences.
Others. Other
flowers, for once and for all.
Finally.

Flowers, which
extend roots—
the question would remain
what for.

Vogel am leeren Winterhimmel

Er durchquert
was?
Da ist ein leerer Raum
oder genaugenommen
etwas Grundloses
ein Klischee.
Langsam
langsam
treibt er weg
ohne voranzukommen.

Bird in the Empty Winter Sky

He crosses
what?
An empty space is there
or more exactly
something groundless
a cliché.
Slowly
slowly
he drifts away
without getting ahead.

Er lobt die Suppe

Wenn er sie anschaut
ist es schon zu spät.
Er weiß es.
Die wenigen Haare
um ihre Brustwarzen
hindern nicht, es nochmals

zu versuchen.

He Praises the Soup

When he looks at her
it's already too late.
He knows it.
The few hairs
around her nipples
don't stop him from

trying again.

Jemand

Leere Räume
aber da
ist wer.
Ich nicht.

Es ist noch
weniger
es ist
gering.

Ich bin
nicht da.
Einmal hätte
es so sein

können, um
da zu bleiben
nicht weit
entfernt.

Das war noch
nicht genug.
Ich stand
auf, um fort

zu gehen.
Es war, als
hätte einer
gesagt: bleib.

Someone

Empty rooms
but someone
is there.
Not me.

It is still
less
it is
very little.

I am
not there.
Once it
could have

been so, in
order to stay there
not far
away.

That was still
not enough.
I stood
up, in order

to go away.
It was as though
someone had
said: stay.

Schlesingers Film

Sie waren
im Anfang
zu glück-
lich. Etwas

weniger, wäre
schon zuviel.
Auch da.
Alles ist

eine Frage der
Beleuchtung.

Schlesinger's Film

In the
beginning
they were
too happy.
Something

less would
have been
too much.
There also.
It's all

a question of
the lighting.

Einmal

Auf einer alten
Photographie stand
irgendeine Frau
neben einem
bekannten Baum.
Vielleicht dachte sie
wie schwer es ist
das zu vergessen
was Blätter hat, grün.

One Time

In an old
photograph stood
some woman
next to a
well-known tree.
Maybe she thought
how hard it is
to forget
what has leaves, green.

Hier nicht

Es war
ein Raum, den
sie langsam
füllte

oder es war
eine Bewegung, die
sie
machte

oder
nur, daß sie da war
und
blieb.

Die Gelegenheit
war
entsprechend der Tageszeit
zu seinen

Gunsten glücklich. Die
Zeit, die
sie blieb
und noch mehr. Die

Bewegung, die
Verwirrung.
Die Art, sie gemeinsam zu
entwirren. Beinahe

hätten sie sagen
können, wir
sind
glücklich.

Not Here

It was
a room which
she slowly
filled

or it was
a movement that
she
made

or
just that she was there
and
stayed.

Considering
the time of day
the opportunity
was to

his advantage. The
time she
stayed
and still more. The

movement, the
confusion.
How together they saw
through the confusion.

They almost
could have said
we're
happy.

Bild von einem Hotel

War es wirklich
das, wonach
ich herumkramte
eine Photographie

zufällig entstanden und
blind
von Licht
in der Erinnerung

war das Hotel viel
dunkler an dem Nachmittag
vollgestopft
mit Gedanken
nicht vom Möwenschrei
isoliert

davon war allerdings
immer viel da
das weiß ich
noch, ohne es zu hören.

Picture of a Hotel

Was it really
that which
I searched for
a photograph

taken accidentally and
blind
with light
in the memory

the hotel was much
darker on that afternoon
stuffed full
with thoughts
not isolated from
the cry of the gulls

there was certainly
enough of that
that I still know
without hearing it.

Alka-Seltzer

Du kannst jetzt
weggehen
oder bleiben
meinetwegen
das ist im Grunde
gleich.

Alka-Seltzer

Now you can
go away
or stay
as far as I’m concerned
it’s basically
the same.

Es war still

Ich stand
müde auf
und wusch
mir mühsam

das Gesicht
und putzte
mir die Zäh-
ne mühsam ab.

Dann ging ich
in die Küche
es war still
und ich dach-

te, wie schön
still es hier
doch ist, wenn
die Kinder tot sind.

It Was Quiet

I woke
up tired
and wearily
washed

my face
and wearily
brushed
my teeth.

Then I went
into the kitchen
it was quiet
and I thought,

how nice and
quiet it is here
when the
children are dead.

Die Konservendose

Die Konserven-
dose, die seit
langem in der
Ecke neben dem

Toilettenbecken
stand, und
der alte Fetzen
Stoff darin, was

hat das zu be-
deuten, fragte
er, sie gab ihm
darauf keine Ant-

wort, und er sah ein
daß sie nicht
antworten woll-
te, weil es schon spät nachts

war und er noch nicht
so müde, um nicht
zu verstehen, daß es
nicht allein nur die-

se Dose war mit
einem alten Lappen
neben dem Klosett.

The Tin Can

The tin can
that's been
standing there
in the corner

by the toilet
for a while now
with the old rag
inside, what's

that for, he
asked her, to
which she had
no answer for

him, and he realized
she didn't want to
answer him, because
it was already so

late, and that he
wasn't tired enough
not to understand
that it wasn't just

this tin can
with the old rag
by the toilet.

Godzilla-Baby

Die Fernseh-
apparate
sind angestellt, aber
nichts passiert. Das

ist das weiße Zittern
das sich
lautlos
ausdehnt. Wir

sitzen in unseren kleinen
schwarzen Gehäusen
und
warten nackt

auf das Ende, bis
sie
plötzlich
da ist. Das

schwarze Leder glänzt
darunter ist sie nackt.
Und sie
fängt ohne

abzuwarten an zu
lutschen: oooooooooooh,
stöhnt
der Mann auf

und hört nicht mehr, wie
die Polizei
das Haus umstellt. (Die
ersten Schüsse fallen

gerade noch zur
rechten Zeit!) Und sie
verschwindet
wieder in dem

Godzilla-Baby

The tele-
visions
are turned on, but
nothing happens. That

is the trembling whiteness
which
silently
expands. We

sit in our little
black houses
and
wait, naked

for the end, until
suddenly
she
is there. The

black leather glistens
she is naked underneath.
And
without waiting

she begins to
suck: oooooooooooh,
groans
the man

and fails to hear how
the police
have surrounded the house. (The
first shots are fired

at exactly the
right time!) And she
disappears
again in the

weißen Zittern
während
die Hausfrau
von einem Bauchschuß

getroffen, sich auf dem
Teppich vor dem Fernseh-
apparat
krümmt.

trembling whiteness
while
the housewife,
hit in the

stomach, curls up
on the carpet in
front of the tele-
vision.

Das Bild

das sie macht
beim Ausziehen
der Strümpfe.
Ich weiß nicht

sagt sie, ob es
noch Pferdefleisch
zu kaufen gibt. Das
Bild, das sie macht

beim Ausziehen
der Strümpfe, ist
nicht zu beschreiben.

The Picture

that she makes
rolling down
her stockings.
I don't know

she says, if
horse meat is
still available. The
picture that she makes,

rolling down
her stockings, is
indescribable.

Godzilla telefoniert so gern

Er nahm
das
Telefon
zur Hand

und fragte
nach
der Farbe
ihrer Schamhaare

dann sagte er
vergnügt
hier
ist der Tod

sie werden
abgeholt
jetzt
gleich

vom Körper
abgerissen
mitgenommen
und dann

weggeworfen.

Godzilla Telephones so Gladly

He took
the
telephone
in his hand

and asked
about
the color
of her pubic hairs

then he said
cheerfully
this
is Death

you will
be
picked up
immediately

your body
dismembered
removed
and then

thrown away.

Wichtig

Der Zeigefinger ist wichtig.
er weist die Richtung

meistens auf eine Stelle
die behaart ist, eine zahnlose

kleine Öffnung, aus der unter
Umständen wieder etwas Flüssig-

keit herauskommt, versteckt in
einer kleinen weißen Hose, die

sich schnell ausziehen läßt.

Important

The index finger is important.
it shows the direction

usually to a place
covered with hair, a toothless

little opening, which, under
certain circumstances, emits a little

fluid again, hidden away
in tiny white panties, which

can be taken off quite quickly.

Godzilla und der Vogel

Ein Vogel ist kein Selbst-
bedienungsautomat, auch
kein Gummitier, sagte er

aber als ich ihn dort
hüpfen sah ohne wegzu-
fliegen, wußte ich, daß

er „piep“ machen würde
wenn ich ihm auf den Kopf
träte. Und der Vogel machte

„piep!“

Godzilla and the Bird

A bird is not a self-
service-automat, nor is it
a rubber animal, he said

but when I saw him there
hopping about without
flying away, I knew that

he'd go "peep" if I were
to step on his head.
And the bird went

"peep!"

Französisch

Oft
sind es nur drei, vier
Worte, als ob es sich

schon nicht mehr lohne
weiterzureden
sondern nur noch

dazustehen und
den Rücken
hinzuhalten

damit man ihr den
Büstenhalter
aufhaken kann

die Stuyvesant
wird aufgeraucht
die Kippe riecht

wie Zigarettenkippen
riechen, denkt sie
wie heißt das auf

französisch?

French

Often
it's just three or four
words, as though it

already wasn't worth it
to go on talking
but rather just

to stand there
with her
back turned

so that one
could unhook
her bra

the cigarette
is smoked
the butt smells

like cigarette butts
smell, she thinks
how do you say that

in French?

Godzillas Ende

Sie kommt und ist da, endgültig.
Es wird später, als man erwartet
hat. Der Ofen geht aus. Ein Geräusch
von einem schweren Fallen ist

draußen zu hören, aber wir sind
drinnen und spüren es nicht. Dann
kommt etwas anderes und ist
dasselbe. Der Ofen geht wieder

aus. Dasselbe Warten. Es wird spät.
Kein Geräusch ist mehr zu hören, aber
wir sind noch da. Die Beleuchtung der
Tankstelle an der Ecke ist schon

lange erloschen. Der Ölofen ist
ausgebrannt. Wir sitzen wieder auf
unseren Stühlen, bis wir umfallen
und das Geräusch von einem schweren

Fallen von neuem draußen zu hören
ist. Später steht sie auf und sagt
„das ist das Ende!" Es ist das Ende.

Godzilla's End

She arrives and is there, for good.
It's getting later than one had
expected. The stove goes out. The sound
of something heavy falling can be

heard outside, but we're still
inside and don't notice it. Then
there's something else and it's
the same. The stove goes out

again. The same waiting. It's getting late.
There's no more sound to be heard, but
we're still there. The lights at the
gas station on the corner have

long since gone out. The oil stove is
burned out. We sit on our chairs
again, until we fall off and the
sound of something heavy falling

can be heard again outside.
Later on she stands up and says
"This is the end!" It is the end.

Chiquita-Banana-High

Die endlose Variation von Blumen
wenn es Blumen sind, aber es sind

keine Blumen. Es ist Papier. Es ist
Geschrei. Es ist ein kleiner Augen-

blick, in dem sich nichts bewegt.
Wir sehen, wie die Läden um halb

sieben jeden Tag von neuem schließen
und es wird ganz still. Der Schnee

fällt auf uns und bedeckt uns ganz.
Jetzt sind wir beide völlig naß.

Chiquita-Banana-High

The endless variations of flowers
when they're flowers, but they're

not flowers. It's paper. It's
screaming. It's a small moment

in which nothing moves. We see
how the stores close up at six-

thirty every day again, and it
becomes very quiet. The snow

falls on us and covers us totally.
Now we're both completely wet.

Die rote Farbe

ist nur eine rote
Farbe, zum Beispiel
der Wasserbehälter
eines Spülklosetts

wenn der plötzlich
rot gestrichen wird
und du bist nicht
da, oder ein paar

rote Flecken auf der
Haut, dann bist du
plötzlich wieder da
und kannst nichts

dafür. Ich meine den
dünnen Stich in der
Seite, wenn du weg-
gehst, und den dünnen

Stich, wenn du wie-
derkommst, ich könnte
auch sagen, so ist es
nicht. Aber der Was-

serbehälter bleibt rot
angestrichen und ich
krieg vorerst die Farbe nicht
mehr von den Fingern ab
ob du nun da bist oder nicht.

The Red Paint

is just a red
color, for example
the water tank
of a toilet

when it's suddenly
painted red
and you're not
there, or a couple

of red spots on the
skin, then you're
suddenly there again
and can't do anything

about it. I mean the
slight pain in the
side when you leave
and the slight pain

when you return,
I could also say
it's not like
that. But the water

tank remains painted
red and I can't get
the paint off of my
fingers whether
you're there or not.

Noch einmal

Meine Frau
auf einem
Bein, nackt

das andere
Bein auf
den Bade-
wannenrand

aufgestützt
fragt nach
der Uhrzeit
wie spät

und ich sehe
den kleinen
Fleck Haar

zwischen ih-
ren Schenkeln
für sie eine
Stelle wie

jede andere
zum Waschen
und denke
warum nicht

während sie
noch einmal
fragt, nackt

das Standbein
gewechselt.

Once Again

My wife
on one
leg, naked

the other
leg supported
on the rim
of the bath

tub, asks
me what
time it is
how late

and I see
the small
spot of hair

between her
thighs that
for her is
just another

place to
wash and
think
why not

while she
asks yet
again, naked

now on her
other leg.

Liedchen

O
fick mich
fick mich
schnell

und er
fickte sie
fickte sie
schnell

hinter
einem Busch?
Es gab keinen
Busch. Schien

der Mond?
Es gab kein
Licht. Die
Birne war

kaputt.

Song

O
fuck me
fuck me
fast

and he
fucked her
fucked her
fast

behind
some bush?
There was
no bush. Did

the moon shine?
There was no
light. The
bulb was

kaput.

Taube,
von einem Piloten beobachtet

Es gibt
viele
schlimme Dinge

                                        und
immer noch einmal
etwas, das
schlimmer ist

wie diese eine
Taube, die so
viel größer ist

als ein Sperling
und so viel doofer
als ein Sperling

den man nicht sieht
                            von oben.

Pigeon,
Observed by a Pilot

There are
many
terrible things

                                        and
always, yet again,
something that's
still more terrible

like this single
pigeon, which is
much bigger than

a sparrow
and much stupider
than a sparrow

which one doesn't see
                    from above.

Eine übergroße Photographie von Liz Taylor

Ich trinke meinen Kaffee wie jeder Kaffee trinkt
aber die Bilder sind anders.
Der eine denkt an irgendetwas
                                        und ich denke
an irgendetwas, Liz Taylor lächelt immerzu.
Wenn es etwas gibt, das sich noch lohnt, dann

ist es das.
Die Krümmung einer Haarlocke und
die natürliche Kräuselung des

Schamhaars
wie Schamhaar sich in meinen
Träumen kräuselt, es ist schon

                                        spät.
Und noch immer lächelt Liz Taylor
mich an. Was ist das? Nehmen wir an, es

ist nichts
was sich lohnt, dann bleibt dieses von allem übrig
nachdem ich meinen Kaffee ausgetrunken habe.

A Blow-up of Liz Taylor

I drink my coffee like anyone else drinks coffee
but the pictures are different.
Someone thinks about something
                                                  and I think
about something, Liz Taylor still smiling away.
If there's something that's still worthwhile, then

it's this.
The curve of a lock of hair and
the natural curling of

pubic hair
like pubic hair curling
in my dreams, it's already

                                        late.
And Liz Taylor is still smiling
at me. What is this? Let's say

it's nothing
worthwhile, then only this remains
after I've finished drinking my coffee.

Der Mond, der Präsident und die amerikanische Prärie Populäres Gedicht Nr. 11

Der amerikanische
Mond über dem
Kapitol in Washington D.C.
ist ganz aus reinem

Kunststoff, eine
endlose Variation
auf ein altes Thema
wie man deutlich sieht.

Der Präsident
sieht ihn sich
täglich einmal
an und läßt ihn

dann wieder verschwinden.
Einsam über einer Prärie
ganz in der Nähe geht
er aber wieder auf. Dieses

Mal ist es der echte Mond
mit dem Abbild des Prä-
sidenten auf der Rückseite.

The Moon, the President and the American Prairie Popular Poem No. 11

The American
moon over the
capitol of Washington D.C.
is made from pure

plastic, an
endless variation
on an old theme
as one clearly sees.

The president
looks at it
once a day
and then lets it

disappear again.
Alone over a prairie,
quite close, it rises
yet again. This

time it's the real moon
with the image of the pres-
ident on the back side.

Der nackte Fuß von Ava Gardner

ist
ein Alptraum, wenn er sich nicht
wieder aus dem Gedächtnis

entfernen läßt
obwohl ich nie mehr in einen Film
mit Ava Gardner
gegangen bin

nachdem ich einmal
gesehen habe, wie der Stoff
sich teilt

und eine Zehe erscheint.
Es gibt Schlimmeres als Zehen, das
weiß ich

aber es gibt nichts, was
sich mit der Zehe von Ava
Gardner vergleichen läßt.

Ein
Vorhang teilt sich und ich
dringe ein in den

wüsten Traum
aus Chinaseide, Plissee, Tüll
und beiseite

geschleuderten leichten
Sandalen. Sie ist barfuß!
Aber wohin geht die Wärme

wenn sie verfliegt?
Was bedeuten die gespreizten Finger auf
einem Schenkel? Wer erlitt den

The Naked Foot of Ava Gardner

is
a nightmare, when it refuses
to let itself be removed from

your memory
although I never went to a movie
with Ava Gardner
again

after I once
saw how the material
parts

and a toe appears.
There are worse things than toes,
this I know

but there is nothing
that can be compared to
the toe of Ava Gardner.

A
curtain parts and I force
my way into the

chaotic dream
of Chinese silk, pleats, tulle
and carelessly

cast-off leather
sandals. She is barefoot!
But where does the warmth go

when it goes?
What's the meaning of the fingers spread
across the thigh? Who suffered the

tragischen
Unfall, als er zum ersten Mal eintreten
wollte und den Schlüssel nicht fand, der

sonst immer unter der Fußmatte lag, und
wer ist das, der nun halb
entblößt im Flur liegt

ohne zu bluten?
Noch bewegte sich eine Zehe
als ich das Kino für immer

verließ.
Das Gedächtnis ist die eine Seite
die andere Seite erfahren wir nie.

tragic
accident, the first time he wanted to enter
but couldn't find the key that

usually lay under the doormat, and
who is that, now lying
half-naked in the hall

without bleeding?
A toe was still moving as
I left the cinema for

ever.
The memory is the one side
the other side we'll never know.

Wie ein Pilot
Populäres Gedicht Nr. 13

Durch eine völlig
glatte Fläche
ganz aus mono-
chromem Blau segelt

da oben der Pilot.
Man sieht und denkt
das gleichzeitig in
einem Bild zusammen

das mit einem Ruck
verschwindet. Später
sagt man sich, daß
man es selbst gewesen

ist, der dort als
winzig kleiner Punkt
verschwunden ist
wie ein Pilot.

Like a Pilot
Popular Poem No. 13

Through a completely
smooth surface
of totally mono-
chrome blue, sails

the pilot up above.
You see and think
this simultaneously
together in one image

that disappears with
a jolt. Later, you
tell yourself that
it was you,

who, up there as
a tiny dot, has
disappeared
like a pilot.

Brief an Humphrey Bogart, schon weit entfernt

Die Fenster
sind alle
geschlossen. Wenn es schellt
wird nicht geöffnet. Ist

dieses Haus leer?
Es ist Februar, es
ist März, es ist April: ich öffne den

Kühlschrank. Keine Leiche im Haus. Lieber
Humphrey Bogart
deine Vision des
Mannes, der nicht

lacht, einsamer Gast
in einem Haus, das nur noch
aus einer Vorderfront
besteht mitten in Beverly

Hills. Doch das Glas in der Hand
zittert nicht. Es ist Mai, Juni, Juli.
Es ist August, September, Oktober.

Keine Schritte auf dem Kiesweg. Keine
Leiche im Haus. Und alle die Fenster
für immer geschlossen nach dem einen

Schuß.

Letter to Humphrey Bogart, Already Far Away

The windows
are all
closed. No door opens
when it rings. Is

this house empty?
It's February, it's
March, it's April: I open the

refrigerator. No corpse in the house. Dear
Humphrey Bogart
your vision of the
man, who doesn't

laugh, lonely guest
in a house which exists only
as a facade
in the middle of Beverly

Hills. But the glass in the hand
doesn't tremble. It's May, June, July.
It's August, September, October.

No footsteps in the gravel. No
corpse in the house. And all the windows
closed forever after the single

shot.

Ra-ta-ta-ta für Bonnie & Clyde etc.

Wenn man plötzlich auf einem einfachen
weißen Kleid einen Klumpen rotes Gelee
zerplatzen sieht, könnte man an das Ende

denken, aber das Ende ist noch weit.
Der Film läuft weiter und Bonnie läuft
weiter und Clyde läuft weiter und wir

laufen alle mit zwischen den Stuhlreihen
und kommen erst zur Ruhe, wenn auch auf
den einfachen weißen Kleidern der Platz-

anweiserinnen ein roter Klumpen Gelee
zerplatzt. Jetzt haben wir wieder Grund
zu laufen, und wir hören noch, wie der Ton

bei der Schlußszene mit dem Maschinen-
gewehrfeuer voll aufgedreht wird zur Freude
von Bonnie und Clyde, den Platzanweiser-

innen und der ganzen Marmeladenindustrie.

Rat-a-tat-tat for Bonnie & Clyde, etc.

When suddenly one sees a clump
of red jelly splattering on a simple
white dress, one could think about

the end, but the end is still far away.
The film runs on and Bonnie runs
on and Clyde runs on and we all

run together between the aisles
and stop only when we see a
clump of red jelly splattering

on the simple white dresses of the
theater ushers. Now we have a reason
to run again, and we can hear how

during the finale with the machine
gun fire the sound is turned up full,
much to the pleasure of Bonnie and Clyde,

the ushers, and the entire marmalade industry.

Lebenslauf einer Frau

Jeden Morgen derselbe nackte
Körper. Da ist der Rest Milch
in der Flasche, und da sind
Haare im Kamm. Sie zieht sich

ihre Strümpfe an und steht
dann da. Der Tag ist bald schon
wieder aus, und sie steht da in
Strümpfen ganz allein. Wenn sie

noch etwas länger stehenbleibt
wird dieser Milchrest in der
Flasche sauer und die Haare
in dem Kamm werden ganz alt. Ein

Tag vergeht so schnell, und sie
rollt ihre Strümpfe von den
Beinen ab, die wehtun von dem
langen Stehen vor sich selbst

und dem, was alles übrigbleibt
wenn man sich einmal auf der
Stelle rührt, um dann so dazustehen
nackt, mit dem Rest Milch und

all den Haaren dort im Kamm.

Biography of a Woman

Every morning the same naked
body. The last of the milk is
there in the bottle and there are
hairs in the comb. She pulls on

her stockings and then stands
there. Already the day is almost
over again, and she stands there
in her stockings all alone. If she

stands there much longer the
milk in the bottle will go
sour and the hairs in the comb
will become very old. A day

goes by so fast, and she
rolls down the stockings from her
legs which ache from standing so
long there alone by herself

and with all that which remains
when one moves without
moving, in order to stand there
naked, with the rest of the milk and

all those hairs in the comb.

Comic No. 2

Hinter den
Wänden von
Gotham-City

wird schwer
gewichst.
Jeder für sich
und Batman und
Robin für uns alle.
Doch noch ist der
Kampf nicht
entschieden.

Der Joker
tritt auf

mit einer neuen
Lutschtechnik.
Die gibt er
Batman als
dreidimensionales
Rätsel auf.
Und oben über
Gotham-City
erscheint

ein riesiges
Ding anstelle

des üblichen
Batsymbols.
Schon will
Batman aufgeben
und sich auch
in die eigenen
vier Wände
zurückziehen
um als Bruce

Comic No. 2

Behind the
walls of
Gotham City

some serious
jerking off
is going on.
Each for himself
and Batman and
Robin for all of us.
But the fight is
not yet decided.

The Joker
shows up

with a new
suck-technique.
He gives this
to Batman
in the form of a
three-dimensional riddle.
And high above
Gotham City
there appears

a giant
Thing instead

of the usual
Bat-symbol.
Already Batman
wants to give up
and retire to
the safety
of his own
four walls
to be Bruce

Wayne vor dem
Fernsehen zu
wichsen, aber

er hat Robin
dabei vergessen

der im letzten
Moment sagt
nein, Batman
laß deine
Bathose an
ich fick
durch den
Batstoff
und du wirst
nichts anderes
spüren als
Suppe, die dir

hinten
reinläuft.

Danach braucht
man nicht mehr
zu Abend
zu speisen.
Das Spiel ist
zuletzt doch
noch gewonnen.

Wayne sitting
in front of the TV
beating off, but

he's forgotten
about Robin
who, at the
very last minute
says no, Batman,
leave your
Bat-pants on
I can fuck you
right through the
Bat-material
and you won't
feel anything
other than
soup

dribbling into you
from behind.

After that
no one has to
eat dinner
at night.
At last
the game
is indeed won.

Der Dreh

Wenn seine Frau
oder eine Frau Nein sagt
ist es schon ein andrer

Tag, und ein Mann
kommt herein
und sieht durch den

Türspalt
sie dort
stehen, allein in dem

großen Zimmer, ein
weißes Ding
das sich nicht

viel bewegt
und dann
fragt, wer ist da

ohne daran zu denken
daß es ein ganz
andrer Mann sein könnte

der sie so dastehen
sieht und nicht
mehr antworten will.

Sie kümmert
es nicht, daß
einer so dastehen kann

und nichts sagt
während sie
fortfährt, das

weiße Ding zu sein
nur weil sie gerade
sich umzieht, um

The Turn

When his wife
or another woman says no
it's already another

day, and a man
comes in and
through the half-

open door
sees her standing
there, alone in the

large room, a
white thing
which doesn't

move much
and then
asks, who is there

without thinking
that it could be
a totally different man

who sees her standing
there and doesn't
want to answer any more.

It doesn't worry
her that
someone can stand there

and say nothing
while she
continues to

be that white thing
just because she happens
to be changing her clothes

sofort eine ganz
andre Frau
sein zu können

für jemand anderes
der sie dann ansieht
und versteht.

Er könnte es
aber nicht
noch einmal

und schreibt: „alles
Liebe, der Gasmann.“
Er öffnet die Backofenklappe

und kriecht ganz hinein.

in order to immediately
become a totally
different woman

for someone else who
then looks at her
and understands.

But he
couldn't
do it again

and writes: "With
love, the Gas Man."
He opens the oven door

and crawls all the way in.

Und

jetzt ist es
schon spät

das Licht fällt
weg, ohne daß
etwas anderes

an dessen Stelle
tritt, keine
Musik im Radio

keine Musik, aber
irgendwo sitzt
noch einer und

funkt irgend-
welche Zeichen
in die Luft

klarer als sonst.
Ich sitze still
am Tisch, froh

daß keiner
kommt und
mich fragt

was das zu
bedeuten hat.
Ich wüßte es

nicht.

And

now it's
already late

the light falls
away, without
anything else

to replace
it, no music
in the radio

no music, but
somewhere someone
is sitting and

sending some kind
of signals
through the ether

clearer than usual.
I sit quietly
at the table, glad

that no one
comes in and
asks me

what that could
possibly mean.
I wouldn't

know.

Künstliches Licht

Wir haben Bilder die sich
„bewegen", und die Bedeutung
ist nicht nur etwas, das sehr

hell ist. Es sind z.B. die
Glühbirnen, die im Dunkeln
verschwinden, und es ist

dieses Muster aus Autounfällen
und „Angst". Ein Junge
liegt ausgestreckt auf dem

Boden unter einer großen
Helligkeit nackt und „bewegt"
seine Hand. Dieser Junge bin

ich. Die Bedeutung einer
solchen Szene ist einfach.
Als ob in der Erinnerung

nur dieses eine „Bild"
wirklich wäre. Ich „tat" das
und später, als ich fertig war

blieb diese „Bewegung" zurück. Aus
zu großer Nähe gesehen, verschwinden
die Einzelteile und werden „Angst".

Artificial Light

We have pictures which
"move," and the meaning
is not just something which is

very bright. There are, for example,
light bulbs, which disappear in
the darkness, and there is

this pattern of car accidents
and "angst". A boy lies
stretched out naked on the

ground beneath a huge
brightness and "moves"
his hand. This boy is

me. The meaning of
such a scene is simple.
As though in the memory

just this single "picture"
was real. I "did" that
and later, when I was finished

just this "movement" remained.
Seen too closely, the details
disappear and become "angst".

Kälter

Es wird kälter
sagte er und

schaltete das
Zimmerlicht an.

Der Raum blieb
dunkel. Und die

Frau dort in dem
Unterrock bewegte

sich etwas. Sie
fror vielleicht

nicht einmal, bis er
dann zu ihr kam

um ihr zu sagen
wie kalt das

alles ist, später.

Colder

It's getting colder
he said and

switched on the
light in the room.

The room remained
dark. And the

woman there in the
slip moved

a little. Maybe
she wasn't

even cold, until
he came to her

to say how
cold it

all is, later.

Alltägliche Musik

Eine ausgedachte
Entfernung,

die es nicht gibt:

eines Morgens kam ich mit irgend etwas nach
Haus zurück,

jetzt

steht es auf der Fensterbank, und ich komme
ins Zimmer, ich wasche mir die Hände, ich trockne
mir die Hände ab,

ich gehe wieder raus.

„Warum" ist eine
Frage,

die nur ein Idiot beantworten könnte, und er
wird sie beantworten,

wenn er um die Ecke
eines solchen
Bildes blickt,

kühl

und

beherrscht.

Ich komme nach Haus, gehe zur Fensterbank,
die Fensterbank ist leer.
Ich selbst
in der Entfernung
mitten im Tageslicht.

Everyday Music

An imagined
distance,

that doesn't exist:

one morning I came back home with
something,

now

it sits on the windowsill, and I come
in the room, I wash my hands, I
dry my hands,

and go out again.

"Why" is a
question

that only an idiot could answer, and
answer it he will,

when he looks
around the corner
of such a picture,

cool

and

collected.

I come home, go to the windowsill,
the windowsill is empty.
My self
in the distance
surrounded by daylight.

Unter Glas

Herr Joseph Beuys,
Künstler,

schneidet sich die Fingernägel und trägt sie
zu einer Ausstellung, wo jeder sie

unter Glas

betrachten
kann.

Wie wäre es, wenn seine Hand öffentlich
einem Hund

an einem
schönen, hellen
Vormittag

„Hundefutter“

hinhielte und dabei den schwarzen Filzhut
ziehen würde:

„bon appetit,
Hund!“

und

der Hund
verreckt.

Under Glass

Herr Joseph Beuys,
Artist,

trims his fingernails and takes them to
an exhibition, where everyone can

observe them

under
glass.

How would it be, when publicly his hand
offered a dog

on a
beautiful, luminous
morning

"dog food"

and while doing so doffed his black
felt hat:

"bon appetit,
dog!"

and

the dog
drops dead.

Nachmittags

Die Zeitungsausschnitte, die sie mit Unfällen und Selbstmorden umgeben, haben ihren Geruch verloren. Er wacht mitten unter ihnen auf und blickt auf die Uhr, die, während er schlief, umgefallen ist. Er öffnet das Fenster... Draußen ist es inzwischen nicht heller geworden, und die Kopfschmerztabletten „warten“ in dem braunen Glas auf dem Bord vor dem Toilettenspiegel. Das ist der gemeinsame Traum vom Haushalt, dem ein Mann und eine Frau verfallen sind. Beide werden sie eines Tages wissen, daß der Geruch verschwunden ist. Sie stehen am Fenster und sehen auf ihren Sohn herunter, der sein blutendes linkes Bein nach sich zieht.

Afternoons

The cut-out newspaper articles, which surround them with accidents and suicides, have lost their smell. He wakes up underneath them and looks at the clock, which, while he slept, had fallen over. He opens the window... Outside it hasn't become any lighter in the meantime, and the aspirin tablets are "waiting" in the brown bottle on the shelf by the bathroom mirror. That is the collective dream of the household, to which a man and a woman have succumbed. One day both of them will know, that the smell has disappeared. They stand at the window and look down at their son, who drags his bloody left leg behind him.

Fotos 1, 2

Die Tiere waren unruhig. Vielleicht, weil
der Platz zu ruhig war. Sie redeten. Nun waren
sie älter geworden und mußten sterben.

Was geht in deinem Verstand vor? Eine Sonne
schlägt rein und setzt die alte Kulisse in Brand.
Ich lebe gern und schaue mir an, wie sie alle

leben. Das ist ganz leicht. Hier hast du den
Fahrschein. Weiter weg kommen die Wellen,
heran. Auf dem Boden liegt Stroh. Darüber

balanciert die Tänzerin, nackt, an Armen
und Beinen, mit blaßblauen Augen. Sie kassiert
später dazu. Ihr Fell ist weich, braun und

lang. Eine Mundharmonika spielte. Die Ebene
davor flammte auf. Ich habe sie gesehen,
und das wars. Der Platz ist inzwischen

saubergeweht. Eine Figur schob den
Kinderwagen voll Zeitungen darüber, kleiner
als der Schatten. Mir schien das ein Ende

zu sein, aber ich hatte mich selber getäuscht.
Die Tiere brannten aus und starben zwischen
den Häusern. Die Häuser sind jetzt leer.

An den Wänden hängen die Bilder, die
keiner mehr berührt. Die Apparate sind
abgestellt. Es ist wieder ruhig geworden,

und ich gehe in dem Sonnenlicht
über den Asphalt, wo sie sind.

Photos 1, 2

The animals were restless. Probably because
the square was too quiet. They spoke. Now they
had become older and had to die.

What goes on in your reasoning? A sun
beats down and sets the old scenery on fire.
I'm glad to be alive and I watch how the others

live. That's very easy. Here you have the
ticket. Farther away the waves are
approaching. On the ground lies straw. Up above

the dancer is balancing, naked, on arms
and legs, with pale blue eyes. Later she
cashes in as well. Her fur is soft, brown and

long. A harmonica was playing. The plains
flamed up in front. I've seen them,
and that was all. The square is meanwhile

swept clean. A figure pushed a
baby carriage full of newspapers by, smaller
than the shadow. It seemed to me to be

an end, but I had fooled myself.
The animals burned out and died between
the houses. The houses are now empty.

On the walls hang the pictures which
no one touches anymore. The apparatuses are
turned off. It's become quiet again,

and I walk into the sunlight,
across the asphalt, where they are.

Ein Gedicht

Hier steht ein Gedicht ohne einen Helden.
In diesem Gedicht gibts keine Bäume. Kein Zimmer
zum Hineingehen und Schlafen ist hier in dem
Gedicht. Keine Farbe kannst du in diesem

Gedicht hier sehen. Keine Gefühle sind
in dem Gedicht. Nichts ist in diesem Gedicht
hier zum Anfassen. Es gibt keine Gerüche hier in
diesem Gedicht. Keiner braucht über einen Zaun

oder über eine Mauer in diesem Gedicht zu klettern.
Es gibt in diesem Gedicht hier nichts zu fühlen.
Das Gedicht hier kannst du nicht überziehen.
Es ist nicht aus Gummi. Kein weißer Schatten

ist in dem Gedicht hier. Kein Mensch kommt
hier in diesem Gedicht von einer Reise zurück.
Kein Mensch kommt in diesem Gedicht hier atemlos
die Treppe herauf. Das Gedicht hier macht keine

Versprechungen. In dem Gedicht stirbt auch keiner.
In diesem Gedicht spürst du keinen Hauch. Es gibt
keinen Laut der Freude in dem Gedicht hier. Kein
Mensch ist in dem Gedicht hier verzweifelt. Hier

in dem Gedicht ist es ganz still. Niemand
klagt in diesem Gedicht. Niemand redet hier
in dem Gedicht. Hier in diesem Gedicht schlagen
sich auch keine Arbeiter wund. Das Gedicht hier

steht einfach nur hier. Es enthält keine Schlüssel
zum Aufschließen von Türen. Es gibt keine Türen
in diesem Gedicht. Das Gedicht hier ist ohne
Musik. Es singt keiner in diesem Gedicht, und

keiner macht hier in diesem Gedicht jemanden
nach. Keiner schreit hier in dem Gedicht, flucht,
fickt, ißt und nimmt ein Rauschmittel. Es gibt in
diesem Gedicht keine bombastische Ausstattung

A Poem

Here stands a poem without a hero.
In this poem there are no trees. No room
to go into and sleep in is here in this
poem. You can't see any color here

in this poem. No feelings are
in this poem. Nothing is in this poem
that you can touch. There are no smells
here in this poem. No one needs to climb

over a fence or a wall in this poem.
There is nothing here in this poem to feel.
This poem here is not one you can wear.
It's not made of rubber. No white shadow

is in this poem here. No one here in
this poem comes back from a trip.
No one in this poem comes breathless
up the stairs. This poem here makes no

promises. In this poem no one dies either.
In this poem you feel no breath. There is
no cry of pleasure in this poem here. No one
in this poem is in despair. Here

in this poem it is completely quiet. No one
complains in this poem. No one talks here
in this poem. Here in this poem no workers
work themselves sore. This poem here

simply stands here. It contains no key
with which to open a door. There are no doors
in this poem. This poem here is without
music. No one sings in this poem, and

no one in this poem imitates anyone
else. No one screams here in this poem, curses,
fucks, eats or takes drugs. There are no
bombastic furnishings in this poem

für dich. Das Gedicht hier geht nicht, liegt nicht,
schläft nicht, es kennt keinen Tag, es kennt keine
Nacht. Du brauchst hier in diesem Gedicht keine
Rechnungen zu Bezahlen. Es gibt keinen Hausbesitzer

in dem Gedicht hier, der die Miete erhöht. Es gibt
keine Firmen in diesem Gedicht. Es gibt in dem
Gedicht keinen Staat Kalifornien. Es gibt kein
Oregano in dem Gedicht. In diesem Gedicht gibts

kein Meer. Du kannst in dem Gedicht hier nicht
schwimmen. Das Gedicht, das hier steht, enthält keine
Wärme, das Gedicht enthält keine Kälte. Das Gedicht
hier ist nicht schwarz, es hat keine Fenster und

kennt keine Angst. Das Gedicht hier zittert
nicht. Das Gedicht hier ist ohne Spiegel. In diesem
Gedicht gibts auch kein Spiegelei. Einen Supermarkt
gibt es hier in diesem Gedicht nicht. Das Gedicht,

das du hier liest, hat keine Titten und keine Fohse,
das Gedicht hier ist völlig körperlos. Keiner stöhnt
hier in dem Gedicht. Das Gedicht blutet nicht, es
verschweigt nichts, das Gedicht hat keine Regel,

das Gedicht ist kein Zitat, für keinen. Hier in
diesem Gedicht findet niemand einen Pfennig,
und hier in diesem Gedicht fährt kein Mensch mit
einem Auto. Keine Reifen quietschen um die Ecke.

In diesem Gedicht lutscht niemand zärtlich an
einem Schwanz. Es gibt hier in dem Gedicht keine
Lampen. Das Gedicht ist kein gelber Schal. Das
Gedicht, auf das du hier schaust, hustet nicht.

Hier in dem Gedicht kannst du nicht küssen.
Hier in diesem Gedicht wird auch nicht gepißt. Du
kannst mit diesem Gedicht nichts anfangen. Das
Gedicht besteht aus lauter Verneinungen. Die

for you. This poem here doesn't walk, doesn't lie,
doesn't sleep, it knows no day, it knows no
night. You don't need to pay any bills
here in this poem. There is no landlord

in this poem who raises the rent. There are
no companies in this poem. There is no
state of California in this poem. There is no
oregano in this poem. In this poem there is

no ocean. You can't swim here in this poem.
This poem, which stands here, contains no
warmth, this poem contains no coldness. This poem
here is not black, it has no windows and

knows no fear. This poem here does not
tremble. This poem here is without a mirror. In this
poem there is also no fried egg. No supermarket
is here in this poem. The poem that

you're reading here has no tits and no cunts,
this poem here is completely bodiless. No one moans
here in this poem. This poem doesn't bleed, it
has no secrets, this poem has no rules,

this poem is not a quotation, for no one. Here in
this poem no one finds a penny,
and here in this poem no one drives
a car. No tires screech around the corner.

In this poem no one sucks tenderly on
a cock. There are no lamps here in this
poem. This poem is not a yellow scarf. This poem,
which you're looking at, doesn't cough.

Here in this poem you can not kiss.
Here in this poem no one pisses. You
can't do anything with this poem. This
poem consists of nothing but negations. The

Verneinungen in diesem Gedicht werden immer mehr.
Hier gibts keinen Kiff in dem Gedicht. In diesem
Gedicht lacht kein Mensch. Das Gedicht kennt keine
Arbeit. Niemand sieht in diesem Gedicht Fernsehen.

Das Gedicht trägt keine Uhr. Das Gedicht ist nicht
zeitlos. Es braucht soviel Zeit, wie du brauchst,
um das Gedicht hier zu lesen. Kein Wasserhahn
tropft in dem Gedicht hier, und keiner verlangt

in dem Gedicht hier nach Zigaretten. Hier das
Gedicht gibt kein Trinkgeld. Keine Toilette ist
hier in dem Gedicht. Es gibt keine Stadt in diesem
Gedicht. Hier in dem Gedicht wäscht keiner sich die

Füße. In die Schule zu gehen, ist hier in dem Gedicht
nicht nötig. In dem Gedicht leckt auch keiner eine
Möhse. Dein Geschlechtsteil richtet sich hier in
dem Gedicht nicht auf. Du kannst hier in dem Gedicht

dich nicht hinsetzen und denken. Das Gedicht hier
ist nicht der Staat. Es ist nicht die Gesellschaft.
Es ist kein Flipperautomat. Das Gedicht hier hat
keinen Hund. Mit diesem Gedicht kann sich keiner

identifizieren. Keine Polizisten fahren in diesem
Gedicht herum und suchen nach einem Bruch. Eine Kuh
liegt hier in diesem Gedicht nicht. Das Gedicht hier
ist nicht gedankenlos. Das Gedicht hier ist nicht

gedankenvoll. In dem Gedicht erscheint auch kein
Sommertag. Es ist niemals Dienstag in diesem Gedicht,
es gibt keinen Mittwoch in diesem Gedicht, es herrscht
nicht Freitag in diesem Gedicht und kein Donnerstag

fehlt in dem Gedicht hier. Es ist nicht Montag,
Samstag und Sonntag hier in dem Gedicht. Das Gedicht
hier ist nicht die Verneinung von Montag oder
Donnerstag. Das Gedicht hört hier einfach auf.

negations in this poem are steadily increasing.
There is no kif in this poem. In this
poem no one laughs. This poem knows no
work. No one watches television in this poem.

This poem doesn't wear a watch. This poem is not
timeless. It needs as much time as you need
to read this poem here. No water spigot
drips in this poem here, and no one asks

in this poem for a cigarette. Here this
poem gives no tip. There is no toilet
here in this poem. There is no city in this
poem. Here in this poem no one washes their

feet. It's not necessary to go to school here
in this poem. In this poem no one licks a
cunt. Your sex organ doesn't stand up
here in this poem. You can't sit down

and think here in this poem. This poem here
is not the state. It is not society.
It is not a pinball machine. This poem here
has no dog. With this poem no one can

identify themselves. No police drive around
in this poem looking for a crime. A cow
is not lying in this poem. This poem here
is not thoughtless. This poem here is not

thoughtful. In this poem no summer day
appears as well. It's never Tuesday in this poem,
there's no Wednesday in this poem, it's not
Friday in this poem and there's no Thursday

missing in this poem here. It's not Monday,
Saturday or Sunday in this poem. This poem
here is not the negation of Monday or
Thursday. This poem simply stops here.

Aufwachen

An einem fast lichtlosen Tag
ohne sich zu stoßen, etwas kühl

und man muß sich wehren, denke
ich, wasch mir das Gesicht, putze die
Zähne, küsse dich, inmitten der Dinge

die bereits lange vor mir bewegt werden.
Mein Schwanz bewegt sich zu dir in der
Stille durch das Zimmer, neben dem

Frühstückstisch ist meine Hand,
unter deinem Rock, auf der weichen
haarigen Stelle, dazwischen.

Ist das Liebe, aufzuwachen und
als erstes ein gekochtes Ei zu
sehen? Als ob man mit dem Finger

über eine Landkarte geht und findet
eine Stelle, anzuhalten, sich
auszustrecken, und das Sonnenlicht

scheint auf den Körper, wärmt ihn,
ohne ein Wort zu sagen.

Waking Up

on one of those almost lightless days
without bumping oneself, somewhat cool,

and one has to defend oneself, I think,
washing my face, brushing my teeth,
kissing you, in between the things

which are already in motion long before me.
My cock moves toward you in the
silence of the room, next to

the breakfast table is my hand,
under your dress, on the soft
hairy place there between.

Is that love, to wake up and
first look at a hard-boiled egg?
As though with a finger

one traces over a map and finds
a place to stop, to
stretch out, and the sunlight

shines on your body, warms it,
without saying a word.

Improvisation 1, 2 & 3 (u.a. nach Han Shan)

„Niemand weiß, woher Han Shan kam."
Er stieg aus der Ebene auf den
Kalten Berg,

schrieb, „was soll ich hier tun?", in den Stein,

die Überschriften fehlten, keine Numerierung

er saß und sah auf den Schnee,

die Erklärungen, „Fußnoten," folgten später, erklärten nichts.

Die Kalligraphien in der Kälte, weiß,
das Anschauen des Steins, das Vergessen

der Erinnerungen, was

eine Leistung ist. Er schrieb, „der Wissende
hat keinen Pfennig," als er wieder

überrumpelt
wurde vom Verlangen, den Berg
zu verlassen, geplagt von der „Kondolation der Fliegen"

&, als er das Zimmer ausfegte, war er zufrieden.

2.

Klack, klack: die Gesellschaft
ist das Abstrakte,

du hörst die vielen
Geräusche die Schuhe,

es ist dasselbe
unendliche Geräusch,

(„alle gaffen
mich an, seit ich den
Weg verlor")

(„die Personen der
Handlung sind frei erfunden,
dasselbe gilt für
die Handlung")

Improvisation 1, 2 & 3 (after Han Shan)

"No one knows from where Han Shan came."
He climbed down from the plateau on
Cold Mountain,

wrote, "What should I do here?" in the stone,

there were no titles, no numbers

he sat there and looked at the snow,

the explanations, "footnotes," came later, explained nothing.

The calligraphy in the coldness, white,
the staring at the stone, the forgetting

of memories, which is

an achievement. He wrote, "The wise man
has not a penny," as he was again

caught by surprise
with the desire to leave
the mountain, troubled by the "condolence of the flies,"

&, as he swept out the room, he was contented.

2.

Clack, clack, the society
is the abstract,

you hear the many
sounds of the shoes

it's the same
endless noise

("everyone
stares at me, since I lost
the way")

("the persons in the
story are fictitious, that
goes for the
story as well")

das die Welt erfüllt, überall, wo du bist.
Und, sagen wir, noch einmal: „plötzlich"
als du die Kurve nahmst,
aus der Stadt herausfuhrst,
nachts auf der Autobahn,
und die Lichterketten zu Ende
waren, hast du's gewußt,

klack, klack (wie Chachacha)

(„gibts was zu
freuen, freue dich
daran")/wenn erst
Unkraut durch den
Schädel sprießt
etc.)

die Wirkung. Und wirklich
ist schwierig, das nicht länger anzusehen,
sondern einzelnes.

3.

Ein Lied zu singen
mit nichts als der Absicht,
ein Lied zu singen,

ist eine schwere Arbeit,
wie vor dem Schnee bedeckten
Berg zu sitzen,

ihn jahrelang, ohne
Ablenkung, anzuschauen und
dann, eines Tages,

mit einem einzigen
Strich weißer Tusche
auf das weiße Papier

zu setzen, daß jeder
sieht der Berg ist
absolut leer.

which fills the world, wherever you are.
And, let's say, once again: "suddenly"
as you took the curve
driving out of the city,
night on the autobahn,
and the chains of lights came
to an end, you knew

clack, clack (like cha-cha-cha)

the effect. And really,
it's difficult not to see that anymore,
but rather the oneness.

("if there's something
to be happy about, be happy
about it")/ when finally
weeds sprout through
your skull
etc.)

3.

To sing a song
with no other purpose
than to sing a song,

is a hard job,
like sitting before the
snow covered mountain,

for years, without
distraction, staring, and
then, one day,

with a single
stroke of white ink
on the white paper,

so placed that everyone
sees that the mountain
is completely empty.

Die Orangensaftmaschine

dreht sich & Es ist gut, daß der Barmann
zuerst auf die nackten Stellen eines
Mädchens schaut, das ein Glas kalten

Tees trinkt. „Ist hier sehr heiß,
nicht?“ sagt er, eine Frage, die
den Raum etwas dekoriert,

was sonst? Sie hat einen kräftigen
Körper, und als sie den Arm
ausstreckt, das Glas auf

die Glassplatte zurückstellt,
einen schwitzenden, haarigen
Fleck unterm Arm, was den Raum

einen Moment lang verändert, die
Gedanken nicht. Und jeder sieht, daß
ihr’s Spaß macht, sich zu bewegen

auf diese Art, was den Barmann
auf Trab bringt nach einer langen
Pause, in der nur der Ventilator

zu hören gewesen ist wie
immer, oder meistens, um
diese Tageszeit.

The Orange Juice Machine

goes around & it's good that the bartender
first looks at the parts of bare skin
of a girl who's drinking a glass of

iced tea. "It's pretty hot here,
eh?" he asks, a question which
decorates the room somewhat,

what else? She has a muscular
body, and as she reaches out
her arm, setting the glass

back on the glass counter,
a sweaty, hairy spot
under her arm, which

momentarily changes the room,
but not the thoughts. And
everyone sees, she likes to move

like this, which gets the bartender
going after a long pause,
in which only the fan

was to be heard, like
always, or usually,
at this time of day.

Einen jener klassischen

schwarzen Tangos in Köln, Ende des
Monats August, da der Sommer schon

ganz verstaubt ist, kurz nach Laden
Schluß aus der offenen Tür einer

dunklen Wirtschaft, die einem
Griechen gehört, hören, ist beinahe

ein Wunder: für einen Moment eine
Überraschung, für einen Moment

Aufatmen, für einen Moment
eine Pause in dieser Straße,

die niemand liebt und atemlos
macht, beim Hindurchgehen. Ich

schrieb das schnell auf, bevor
der Moment in der verfluchten

dunstigen Abgestorbenheit Kölns
wieder erlosch.

One of Those Classic

black tangos in Cologne, end of
the month of August, when the summer

is already so dusty, just after the stores
have closed, coming out of the open door

of a dark bar which belongs
to a Greek—to hear that, is almost

a wonder: for one moment a
surprise, for one moment

a sigh of relief, for one moment
a pause in this street,

which no one loves, and which leaves one
breathless when passing through. I

quickly wrote that down, before
the moment was extinguished in the cursed

hazy deathly-numbness of Cologne
once again.

Ein anderes Lied

„Ich habe keinem
mehr etwas zu sagen."

Warum öffnet sie dann
den Schrank und sucht nach
ein paar Strümpfen?

Das sind die alten Melodien,
die jeder anders versteht.

Laß eine Ameise über den Arm
kriechen. Hörst du, wie sie singt? Nein,
das ist ein Geräusch auf der

anderen Straßenseite. Es sind immer die
selben Trampelpfade der Liebe, die man geht.
Einer singt im Unterhemd auf dem Balkon,

der Balkon ist nicht zu sehen. Das
Nachmittagslicht fällt schräg
zwischen die Häuser.

Die Wind bewegt lautlos die
Fransen der verblichenen
Markise. Der Augenblick

wurde lautlos gelb, verblich. Es
gibt eine große Anzahl Augenblicke,

die so gespenstisch sind, daß
man nicht einmal erschrickt,

z.B. alle Straßen sind leer
und die Ampeln funktionieren.

Nun bist du schön.

Was wird sie
dann sagen?

„Wozu?"

A Different Song

"I have nothing else
to say to anyone."

So why does she open
the closet and look for
a pair of stockings?

These are the old melodies,
which everyone understands differently.

Let an ant crawl over
your arm. You hear how it sings? No,
that's a sound on the

other side of the street. It's always the
same old paths of love which one follows.
Someone in an undershirt sings on the balcony,

the balcony is not visible. The
afternoon light falls obliquely
between the buildings.

The wind silently moves the
tassels on the faded
awning. The moment

becomes silently yellow, fades.
There are a great number of moments

which are so uncanny
that one isn't even shocked,

e.g. all the streets are empty
and the stoplights are functioning.

Now you are beautiful.

What will she
say then?

"Why?"

Ein Glas frisches Wasser

& im Schatten einschlafen. Mich kümmert
nicht eine nächste Katastrophe.
Das Rascheln

der Tageszeitung ist nur eine Verwechslung
der Orte, wo die Türen, weit entfernt, zu
geschlagen werden. Das Oberhemd, neu gewaschen,

ist trocken, als ich erwache. Es gilt einfach,
viele gute Augenblicke zu erwischen. Und wer
ist der Idiot, der im Treppenhaus mit Kohlen

spielt? Das ist ein liegengebliebenes Stück
aus dem Traum, das schnell verheizt werden
muß: „Einsamkeit, wo du bist, wächst kein

Grashalm, & keiner gebraucht einen
Lippenstift, einfach aus Lust da
zu sein und schön.“

A Glass of Cold Water

& falling asleep in the shadows. I don't care
about the next catastrophe.
The rustling

of the newspaper is just a confusion
of the places where the doors, far away, are
slammed shut. The shirt, newly washed,

is dry when I wake up. It's simply a matter
of catching many good moments. And who
is the idiot playing with coal in the

stairwell? That's a leftover piece
of the dream, which must quickly be burned
up: "Loneliness, where you are, no blade

of grass grows, & no one needs a
lipstick, simply out of a desire to
be there and be beautiful."

Einige sehr populäre Songs

wie z.B. Kühe unterm Mond,
friedliche Seelen, die wiederkauen,
Buddhadärme im hohen Gras, versteckt
zwischen kleinen Gehölzen und

gehäuften Büschen im stetigen
Grün, eine praktische schwarz-weiß
gefleckte Metaphysik, gepeinigt von
Sommerfliegen, die an ihrem Speichel

kleben. Der Raum hängt im Innern
ihrer Augen wie eine Zimbel, die
zum Schlachthof läutet. Oder eine
blaue Regentonne im Süden, wo der

Himmel eine endlose Fortsetzung
von Blau ist, halluzinierte Räume
am Tag, aber wirklich. Die Tricks
der Rolling Stones sind aus.

Ich höre Leonard Cohen singen,
there is a war between the men
and the women, why don't you come
on back to the war, it's just be

ginning. Verschiedenes Gras wächst
die Ränder entlang, verzaubertes
Grün. Das Gras wird bewegt, bewegt
sich, und die Jahre kamen alle, wie

immer, hintereinander: auf Wieder
Sehen, schnelle Wolke, auf Wiedersehen,
blauer Himmel im Fensterrahmen, auf
Wiedersehen, getrocknetes Gras,

nackt in der ersten Dämmerung,
auf Wiedersehen. Ein nasser Stachel
Drahtzaun steht da, schiefe Zäune,
auf Wiedersehen, Vorstädte, als ob

Some Very Popular Songs

for example cows beneath the moon,
peaceful souls, ruminating,
Buddha-guts in the high grass, hidden
between small trees and

clumps of brush in the constant
greenness, a practical black-and-white-
spotted metaphysics, tormented by
summer flies which stick to their

saliva. The space hangs inside
their eyes like a gong, which
beckons to the slaughterhouse. Or a
blue rain barrel in the south, where

the sky is an endless continuation
of blue, hallucinated spaces
during the day, but real. The tricks
of the Rolling Stones are over.

I listen to Leonard Cohen singing,
there is a war between the men
and the women, why don't you come
on back to the war, it's just be-

ginning. Various grasses grow
along the edges, enchanted
green. The grass is moved, moves
itself, and all the years came, like

always, one after the other: good-
bye, fast cloud, goodbye
blue sky in the window frames, good-
bye, dried grass,

naked in the first twilight,
goodbye. A wet barbed
wire fence stands there, crooked posts,
goodbye, suburbs, as though

niemand dort lebt, Bruchstücke von
Biografien und Zeitungspapier, das
sinnlose Winken. Manche Zeilen sind
wie das Winken von Kindern aus einem

Zugfenster nachmittags beim Vorüber
Fahren an fremden Städten, beim Vorüber
Fahren an den Mietskasernen mit den
einzelnen Gesichtern an den Fenstern:

wenn alle Bekenntnisse der Welt, die
jemals in den Gerichtshöfen der Welt
abgegeben und aufgeschrieben worden
sind, zusammengestellt würden und

hintereinander vorüberzögen, was
für einen endlosen Jammer gäbe das,
auf der Welt zu sein. Jemand
ruft an, wählt irgendeine

Nummer, und ich höre nur
seinen Atmen, und da ist wieder
die Entfernung, das leise
knisternde Geräusch der

Verwirrung an einem anderen
Ort und sonst nichts da
am Nachmittag. Und wenn du morgens auf
stehst und du starrst auf das Hotel

Frühstück, und du verstehst nicht,
warum du in diesem Hotelzimmer bist,
wo du tatsächlich bist, und du denkst
nach einer fast schlaflosen Nacht,

was du morgens am acht tun kannst,
und dir fällt nichts anderes ein, als
die drei schmutzigen Oberhemden zur
Wäscherei zu bringen, nachdem du schon

no one lives there, fragments of
biographies and newspapers, the
senseless waving. Some lines are
like the waving of children from a

train window while passing through
strange cities in the afternoon, passing
the rows of low-rent apartments with the
single faces at the windows:

if all the confessions in the world
that were ever given and written down
in the courts of the world
were put together and

dragged by one after the other, what
an endless misery it would be
to be in the world. Someone
calls, dials any old

number, and I hear only
their breath, and there again is
the distance, the soft
crackling noise of the

confusion in another
place, and otherwise nothing there
in the afternoon. And in the morning, when
you get up and stare at the hotel

breakfast and you don't understand
why you're in this hotel room,
where you actually are, and you think
about what you can do at eight in the morning

after an almost sleepless night,
and nothing else comes to mind except
to take the three dirty shirts to
the laundry, having already

um sieben Uhr geduscht hast, umarmst
du um neun Uhr dann das Morgenlicht?
Oder sagst du, auf Wiedersehen Morgen
Licht? Und dann hörst du eine Wasser

Toilette rauschen, während du einen
langen Flur entlanggehst, und was
fühlst du dann? Daß alles in Ordnung
ist? Um zehn Uhr ruft jemand an und

erzählt vom Tod, und du machst einen
Witz über den Krebskranken Filmvor
Führer, der seit 25 Jahren in der
Firma ist, und wer im Zimmer ist,

lacht, mit. Wer geht durch die Räume,
fremd, und erinnert sich an die Zeile
aus dem Lied: Grüne Blätter, wie seid
ihr allein? Was für verfluchte einsame

Geschäftsbriefe werden geschrieben.
Die Unterschriften spielen keine Rolle.
Und du singst dein Lied, „Lady, ich hau
ab!" Auch das gehört zu den populären

Songs. Die friedlichen Buddhaseelen
liegen schwarz und weiß gefleckt im
Grünen. Sie kauen unterm gleichen
Licht die sanften Gräser wieder.

2. (für H. S.)

Wo der Rubel in einzelne Kopeken
zerfällt oder der Dollar in Cents,
oder die DMark in Pfennige wie
der Gulden, wo die Lire zerfallen

wie der Franc in Centimes und das
englische Pfund in den Knaster der
spanischen Münzen, wo die Ostmark
in Augenfalten zerbricht und ein

showered at seven, do you
embrace the morning light at nine?
Or do you say, goodbye, morning
light? And then you hear the rush

of a flushing toilet while you
walk along a long hallway and what
do you feel then? That everything is
in order? At ten someone calls and

talks about death, and you make a
joke about the film projectionist with cancer
who's been with the company for 25
years, and whoever else is in the room

laughs as well. Who goes through the rooms,
unfamiliar, and remembers the lines
from the song: Green leaves, how are
you alone? What sort of damned lonely

business letters are being written.
The signatures don't matter at all.
And you sing your song, "Lady, I'm
out of here!" That also belongs to the popular

songs. The peaceful Buddha-souls
lie spotted black-and-white in the
greenness. They chew beneath the same
light the soft green grass again.

2. (for H.S.)

Where the ruble disintegrates into single
kopecks, or the dollar into cents,
or the D-mark into pfennigs like
guilders, where the lira disintegrates

like the franc into centimes and the
English pound into the cheap tobacco of
Spanish coins, where the ostmark
breaks into eye-wrinkles and a

Traktor im Kerzenlicht steht, wo der
schwedische Öre in Versicherungen
zerfällt wie Weltreiche, wo der Stör
in den Flüssen stirbt und der Hering

in der Nordsee, wo die Entfernungen
zwischen den Städten wachsen wie der
Zerfall zwischen den einzelnen Städten,
wo der Yen in den Cruzeiro gewechselt

wird, wo zuviel in die Seife investiert
ist, wo die bulgarischen Konservendosen
in argentinische Tratten verwandelt
werden, zerfallen wie die finnische

Währung, wo Wälder die Flüsse runter
geflößt werden, wo Knochenmehl zu
Kunststoffen wird, wo Summen kopiert
werden, wo die Flußgänse zu Slotys werden

und in schwarzem Aspik eingefroren sind,
wo der Dinar die Kamele antreibt, das
Mais auf den Feldern verfault, zerfallen
wie Zähne, die gewechselt werden, wo der

Peso verreckt, die schwarze Unterwäsche
hebt, zerfallen wie Banderolen, in was
für Münzen die Gesichter auch zerfallen,
in welcher Notdurft, Pisse, Lehmwege, Rast

Räume und Bettlaken, wo die Armee das
Studium der Gedichte finanziert, wo die
technischen Institute die Welt erklären,
das zuckende Herz einer Schildkröte, an

Fäden befestigt, zur Schau gestellt ist,
wo die Lizenzen Grenzen ziehen, zerfallen
in Tierbilder, wo Unterschriften benötigt
werden, Testamente, Konten, wo die Bank

tractor stands in the candlelight, where the
Swedish öre disintegrates into insurance
like world empires, where the sturgeon
dies in the rivers and the herring

in the North Sea, where the distances
between the cities grow like the
disintegration among the single cities,
where the yen is changed into the cruzeiro,

where too much is invested in soap,
where the Bulgarian tin cans
are converted into Argentinean bank
drafts, disintegrating like the Finnish

currency, where forests are rafted
down the rivers, where bone meal
becomes plastic, where sums are
copied, where the geese become zlotys

and are frozen in black aspic,
where the dinar drives the camel, the
corn rots in the fields, decaying
like teeth which will be exchanged, where the

peso dies miserably, the black underwear
rises, disintegrating like revenue stamps into
whichever sort of coins the faces may disintegrate,
into whatever bodily needs, piss, dirt paths, rest

rooms and bed sheets, where the army is
financing the study of poetry, where the
technical institutes explain the world,
the twitching heart of a turtle

hanging from a thread for all to see,
where the licenses set the limits, decomposing
into animal-pictures, where signatures are
needed, testaments, accounts, where the bank

Feiertage zum Aufatmen da sind, die Fahnen
herausgehängt werden, den Tag zu drapieren,
wo das Karbid stank, wo die Flaschen zerplatzten,
wo die Trümmer herumlagen und die Tätowierungen,

Die Konzerne wuchern wie Massenmedien,
die Gesteinsbrocken und Trümmer sind bei
Seite geräumt, der Schmerz und die Trauer
verhökert, zerfallen in Monatsgehälter,

wo gibts noch was zu tun, das Gespenst
der Arbeitslosigkeit treibt sie zusammen,
das Gespenst der Besitzenden, das Gespenst
der Angestellten, wo alle damit beschäftigt

sind, diese Welt zu verwalten, oder was sie
für diese Welt halten, Fälle, zusammengetrieben
in den Büros, aber die Büros zerfallen, wo
die Zimmer viele Türen haben und gläserne

Wände, die Aufzugschächte zerfallen, die
Passagen zerfallen, zertrümmerte Schau
Fenster, Schimmelpilzkulturen, wilde
Vegetation, dazwischen Schaufenster

Puppen, Ratten huschen durch lange
zerfallene Passagen, Ratten durch die
leeren bleichen Korridore der Hochhäuser,
wo die letzen Krüppel noch zusammen

getrieben werden, alle zusammengetrieben,
diese Welt zu verwalten, diese Mauern,
Maschendrahtzäune, Eingänge, die Klassen
Räume, wie zerfallene Swimming Pools,

wie Unterschriften, die zerfallen, wo
nachts in den Hochhausapartments die
Kinder schreien, furchtbar gefesselt
an die Stille, wo die Kinder die Baby

holidays are there for a sigh of relief, to hang
out the flags and decorate the day,
where the carbide stank, where the bottles burst,
where the rubble lay strewn and the tattoos,

the companies proliferate like the mass media,
the chunks of stone and rubble have been
cleared aside, the pain and the sorrow
sold off, decomposed into monthly wages,

where there is still something to do, the specter
of unemployment drives them together,
the ghosts of the owners, the ghosts
of the employees, where all of them are busy

administering this world, or what they consider
to be this world, traps, driven together
in the offices, but the offices disintegrate,
where the rooms have many doors and glass

walls, the elevator shafts disintegrate, the
arcades disintegrate, smashed store
windows, mold spores, wild
vegetation, in between store-window

mannequins, rats scurrying through
long ruined arcades, rats in the
pale empty corridors of the skyscrapers,
where the last cripples are still being

driven together, everyone driven together
to administrate this world, these walls,
cyclone fences, entrances, the class-
rooms like ruined swimming pools,

like signatures which disintegrate, where
nights the children scream in the
apartment towers, dismally bound
to the silence, where the children throw up

Nahrung wieder auskotzen, wo die Körper
nebeneinander im Dunkeln liegen und
onanieren, um in den Schlaf zu kommen,
endlich erschöpft und leer, zerfallen

wie das Gesicht einer Fernsehansagerin
im halbirren Traum, die neue Ankündigungen
macht in verschiedenen Stimmen wie auf
zerkratzen Schallplatten, zerfallen

wie Schillinge, wo aus dem verdrehten
Schmerz Witze in einer Mundart entstehen,
beklatscht von den Reihen, wo die Reihen
endlich zerfallen, wo eine Radiosprecherin

ihren Tampon aus dem haarigen Loch zwischen
den Beinen auf der Toilette der Anstalt
des öffentlichen Rechts zieht, in einer
Pause, wo Gedichte gelesen werden, wo die

Sonntage endlos sind, zerfallen wie kranke
Lungen, wo gesprochen wird, das ist nicht
dein Gesicht, das ist nicht dein Gesicht,
wo die Münzen in Gesichter zerfallen, alte

Gesichter, tote Gesichter, abgehärmt und
häßlich auf den Scheinen, die zerfallen, wo
wir gehen, einfaches Tageslicht glitzert
in den Regenpfützen, glitzert in den

tropfenden Bäumen, Freude, das Erstaunen
der Augen, wo du lachtest, als du deinen
Wohnwagen sahst, das schöne Lachen totalen
Unverständnisses, als du die Wagentür auf

machtest, wo die Schecks die Umgebung
zersetzen, Papier in Nickel zerfiel, zer
fallen wie eine Währung aus schwarzer
Traumschlacke, die bei der nächsten

their baby food again, where the bodies
lie next to each other in the darkness and
masturbate in order to go to sleep,
finally exhausted and empty, decomposing

like the face of a television announcer
in the half-insane dream, who makes new
announcements in different voices like on
scratched records, disintegrating

like shillings, where the twisted
pain becomes jokes in a dialect,
applauded by the ranks, where the ranks
finally disintegrate, where a radio announcer

pulls her tampon out of the hairy hole
between her legs on the toilet in the office
of the National Public Radio during a
pause in which poems are read, where the

Sundays are endless, decayed like sick
lungs, where it is said, that is not
your face, that is not your face,
where the coins disintegrate into faces, old

faces, dead faces, grieved and
hideous on the banknotes which disintegrate,
where we go, simple daylight sparkles
in the rain puddles, sparkles in the

dripping trees, pleasure, the astonishment
of the eyes, when you laughed as you
saw your trailer, the beautiful laughter
of a total lack of understanding as you opened

the car door, where the checks corroded
the surroundings, paper disintegrated into nickel,
decayed like a currency made from black
dream-slag, which crumbles at the

Berührung zerfällt, wo eine Frau keine
andere Möglichkeit hat als vorwärts
durch die Büsche, wo Bolivar in Centimos
zerfällt, wo du vielleicht im Traum bist,

es ist Zeit, daß wir einander mehr Geschichten
erzählen, wo man nicht mit dem Rücken zur
Wand steht, sondern in der offenen Tür, im
Tageslicht, das nicht zerfällt wie die wellige

Ebene mit kreisenden, trägen Hühnergeiern
darüber, schwarze ruhige Bewegungen, klar
in der Luft, wo der Himmel nicht mehr
in das Bild paßt und mit den Wolken

im Fenster weiterzieht. Wer ruft durch
die vereisten Wälder? Wer wandert durch
die verschneiten Säle? Wer friert und
kauert zusammengezogen auf dem endlosen

Umsteigebahnhof, wo die Rupien zerfallen,
umgewechselt in Dirham, Visagen darauf, Wahr
Scheinlichkeitsrechnungen, Hundeknochen,
der Tod eine weiße Erscheinung in einem

weißen unsichtbaren Zelt, Jeepspuren mit
Staubwolken hinter sich herschleppend,
der Tod ist ein ausgetrocknetes Kamel
Gerippe am Wegrand, der Tod ist ein

toter Skunk auf dem Highway, der Tod
ist eine tote Katze auf dem leeren
Parkplatz, der Tod sind die langen
Reihen der Anzüge auf der verchromten

Stange in der nächsten Herrenabteilung,
der Tod ist ein umgeschlagener
Baum, wo die Schattenschuhe liegen, aus
gelatscht, wo die Häuser keine Wände

next touch, where a woman has no
other chance than forward through the
bushes, like Bolivar disintegrating into
centimos, where maybe you're in a dream,

it's time that we tell each other more
stories, where one doesn't stand with their back
to the wall, but rather in an open door, in
the daylight, which doesn't disintegrate like the

wavy plateau with the lethargic chicken hawks
circling above, quiet black movements, clear
in the air, where the sky no longer
fits in the picture and together with the clouds

passes by in the window. Who's calling through
the frozen forests? Who's wandering through
the snowed-in halls? Who's freezing
and huddled together in the endless

transfer station, where the rupees disintegrate,
changed into dirhams, faces upon them,
theories of probability, dog bones,
death a white apparition in a

white invisible tent, Jeep tracks with
dust clouds trailing behind,
death is a dried-up camel
skeleton by the wayside, death is a

dead skunk on the highway, death
is a dead cat on an empty
parking lot, death is the long
rows of suits on the chromed

rack in the next men's department,
death is a chopped down
tree, where the shadow-shoes lie, worn
out, where the houses have no

mehr haben, wo die elektrischen Lichter
in den Zimmern umherwandern, Kernzerfall,
Multiplikationen, Brillengläser, hinter den
Eisblumen am Fenster ist das Buch zugeklappt

und ein Gesicht weint, ein Gehirn wird
geöffnet, der Rausch einer dunkeln, klaren
Winternacht ist mit Sternbildern illuminiert
und stürzt nicht ab, wo der Tod ein ausge

trocknetes Flußbett ist, weißes Geröll
und die Ebene fliegt, du siehst das,
wir sahen sie ausgebreitet, die Ebene,
weiß im Scheinwerferlicht vorüberfliegend,

ich ging zurück in das schnell errichtete
Apartment, die Träume fortführend, die Ebene
weiß, ich starrte in den Aluminiumtopf, auf
den Rest Broccoligemüse unterm Licht,

weiß zieht die Ebene vorüber mit den
leichten Zeichen, die wir machen, wo eine
dreckige, rachitische Klaue eine saubere
Hand ist, die über den Mahagonitisch

streicht, sie hat die vielen Tagträume
ausgeräubert, nun liegt sie rachitisch
verkrümmt auf der sauberen Fläche, wo der
luxemburgische Franc zu malaiischem Dollar

wird, der in kubanische Pesos zerfällt,
wer scheißt Geld aus und läßt einen Wald
absterben, damit er in den Comics erscheint,
massiert am Strand, der mit Fußangeln und

Selbstschüssen, von Hubschraubern bewacht,
markiert ist, wer schleppt seinen Koffer
durch den Busbahnhof, wer wirft eine Münze
in den Fernsehautomaten, wer blättert in

walls anymore, where the electric lights
wander about in the rooms, nuclear decay,
multiplication, optical lenses, behind the
frost patterns on the window the book is shut

and a face cries, a brain is
opened, the exhilaration of a dark, clear
winter night is illuminated by constellations
and does not fall, where death is a dried-

up river bed, white gravel
and the plateaus fly by, you see that,
we saw them spread out, the plateaus,
flying by white in the headlights,

I went back into the hastily constructed
apartment, the dreams continuing, the plateau
white, I stared into the aluminum pot,
at the rest of the broccoli under the light,

the plateau passing by, white, with the
slight indication that we make, where a
dirty, rickety claw is a clean
hand stroking a mahogany

table, having plundered the many
daydreams, now it lies rickety and
crooked on the clean surface, where the
Luxembourgean francs become Malian

dollars, which disintegrate into Cuban pesos,
who is it who shits out money and lets a forest
die so that he can appear in the comics,
massaged on the beach, he with the mantraps

and self-inflicted gunshots, observed by helicopters,
a marked man, who is it who drags their suitcase
through the bus station, who is it who drops a coin
into the TV automat, who is it who skims the

den psychoanalytischen Zeitschriften,
einen Fall zu klären, wer interpretiert
die Welt, wer interpretiert den nächsten
Bauzaun, wer interpretiert das Apartment,

Schatten von Menschen in den Asphalt
gebrannt, Steine mit Menschenschatten zur
Besichtigung freigegeben, Flugaufnahmen der
Landschaft vom Kriegsministerium für Post

Kartengrüsse freigegeben, wer freigibt, glaubt
ein Recht zu haben auf die Einzäunungen,
wo die Piaster Schrott sind, die Poesie ist
kein Wartesaal, worin man übernachtet, müde,

vor sich eine ausgebreitete Tageszeitung
mit dem Gewimmel des Krieges, jedes Wort ist
Krieg, Schrottwörter wie der Tod, zu Herden
zusammengetrieben, ohne Unterscheidungen,

hätte ich mit deiner Frau schlafen
sollen, hätte ich mehr Illustrierten haben
müssen, hätte ich die Spülmaschine benutzen
sollen, hätte ich den Kinoreklamen folgen

müssen, filigranes Grau hypothetischer Fragen,
Ranken, Zementverzierungen, wo die Träume
absterben wie Ebenen, ein Kanister am
Haifisch, der tägliche Blick aus dem

Fenster in diese Seitenstrasse, die du
nicht kennst, wo der Dollar in Kopeken
zerfällt und der Rubel in Cents, wo aus
den Knochen die Peseten gewonnen werden,

doch die Freude ist größer als die
Trauer, die Drachme ist kleiner als die
Lust, zerkleinert zu hundert Lepta, die
bei der nächsten Gelegenheit verschwinden,

psychoanalytical journals in order
to solve a case, who is it who interprets
the world, who is it who interprets the next construction-
site fence, who is it who interprets the apartment,

shadows of people burned into the
asphalt, stones with human shadows
on exhibit, aerial photographs of the
landscape allowed for postcard greetings

by the Minister of War, he who allows, believes
he has the rights for fencing in,
where the piastres are scrap, poetry is
not a waiting room where one stays overnight, tired,

behind a newspaper opened to the
swarming masses of war, every word is
war, scrap-words like death, driven
together in herds, without differences,

should I have slept with your wife,
should I have had more magazines,
should I have used the dish-
washer, should I have followed the movie

posters, filigree-gray hypothetical questions,
tendrils, cement ornamentation, where the dreams
die off like plateaus, a canister on the
shark, the daily view out the

window into this side street, which you
don't know, where the dollar disintegrates
into kopecks and the ruble into cents, where
pesetas are wrung from the bones,

but the pleasure is greater than the
sorrow, the drachma is smaller than the
lust, reduced to a hundred lepta, which
disappear at the next opportunity,

wo aus den Sehnen die türkischen Pfunde
gezogen werden, zerfallen, zerfallen in den Bauten
des 19. & 20. Jahrhunderts in Westdeutschland,
Verlängerungen, Tratten, Obligationen, alles

dasselbe, verhökert, ausgelatscht, geschunden,
noch einmal verhökert vom Fernsehen, von der
Serie, von der Musikbox. Sanftes Gesicht,
du hast inmitten der Menge den zuckenden

Körper gesehen, auf einmal war das
Konzert vorbei, hast du gestammelt, hast
du, wo die Gänge aus Beton sind, geweint,
wo die Boxen dröhnten, wo die Gesichter

in Traumfalten zerbrachen, wo die Stadtpläne
weiße Flecken haben, wo die Farbe Weiß keines
wegs der Tod ist, wo das Hundefell nicht wärmt,
wo die Wege enden, Elfenbeinküste ist ein

fantastisches Wort, Tätowierungen,
Narben, Umzüge, Auszüge, vielen Dank.

3. (Historie)

Heute Nacht dachte ich über die Liebes
Geschichte Adolf Hitlers nach.
Ich sah die Dauerwellen in der Frisur
von Eva Braun. Wieviele deutsche Weiber

sehen heute aus wie das Lächeln von
Eva Braun. Die Fotos vermehren sich.
Ich bin nicht, weiß ich, in einem Foto
geboren worden. Schnee fiel in April,

als ich geboren war, eingehüllt in den
verzierten Decken des Taufrituals.
Der Krieg, ich verstehe nicht, was das
ist, welche Sprache ist wo? Eva Braun

where the Turkish pounds are extracted from
the tendons, decayed, decayed in the buildings
of the 19th & 20th centuries in West Germany,
extensions, bills, obligations, everything

the same, pawned off, worn out, trashed,
pawned off again on television, from the
serial, from the jukebox. Gentle face,
in the middle of the crowd you've seen

the twitching body, suddenly the
concert was over, did you stammer, did
you cry, where the corridors are cement,
where the speaker boxes boomed, where the faces

broke into dream-wrinkles, where the city maps
have white spots, where the color white in no way
means death, where the dog fur fails to warm,
where the ways end, Ivory Coast is a

fantastic name, tattoos,
scars, moving in, moving out, many thanks.

3. (History)

Last night I was thinking about the love
story of Adolf Hitler.
I saw the permanent waves in the hair
of Eva Braun. How many German women

today look like the smile of
Eva Braun. The photos reproduce themselves.
I was not, I know, born in a
photograph. Snow fell in April,

as I was born, shrouded in the
ornamental cloth of the baptism ritual.
The war, I don't understand what that
is, which language is where? Eva Braun

lächelte Adolf Hitler an, das war in
Berlin. Was hat Adolf Hitler zuerst zu
Eva Braun gesagt? Welche Entfernungen
bestehen zu den Dauerwellen auf dem

Foto und der altmodischen Brennschere
für Dauerwellen, die ich später auf einer
Fensterbank liegen sah? Ich dachte in Berlin,
als ich in der Akademie der Künste schlief,

an diese Brennschere für Dauerwellen.
Das Foto war eine Erinnerung, auf die ich
sah. Zwanzig Jahre später sah ich auf ein
fettes Gesicht in der Tages

Zeitung, das in einem Berliner Hotel den
Muckefuck aus Hoteltassen trank, der Titel
war Professor, der Titel war nicht zu identi
fizieren. Eva Braun, war dein Nacken ausrasiert?

Eva Braun, was ist dir zu Sarottischokolade
eingefallen? Adolf Hitler, als du mit dem Pelikan
Malfarbkasten in München gingst, was hast du
gesehen? Die Sütterlinschrift verdarb die

Handschriften. Von den Handschriften sollte
ich lernen. Adolf Hitler war über die Stadt
Pläne geflogen. Eva Braun besah sich im
Kristallspiegel ihre Fotze. Welche Schenkel

Größe hattest du, Eva Braun? Ich kenne Mädchen,
die genauso aussehen wie Eva Braun, die auf
dem Foto wie Eva Braun aussieht. Ich wuchs
auf, betrachtete mein Schamhaar, betrachtete

Brustwarzen, betrachtete das Schilf, Jahre
später betrachtete ich das Bild von Eva Braun.
Im selben Monat wird eine Brust von der
Frau des amerikanischen Präsidenten ab

smiled at Adolf Hitler, that was in
Berlin. What did Adolf Hitler first say
to Eva Braun? Which distances
exist between the permanent waves on the

photo and the old fashioned curling iron
for permanent waves which I saw later
on a windowsill? As I slept in the Academy
of Art in Berlin, I thought about

this curling iron for permanent waves.
The photo was a memory which I looked
at. Twenty years later I looked
at a fat face in the daily

paper, which drank ersatz coffee in a Berlin
hotel from a hotel coffee cup, the title was
Professor, the title was not to be identi-
fied. Eva Braun, was your neck shaved?

Eva Braun, what did you think about the Sarotti
chocolates? Adolf Hitler, as you went through
Munich with your Pelikan watercolors, what did you
see? The Sütterlin script ruined the

handwriting. From the handwriting I was supposed
to learn. Adolf Hitler skimmed over the city
maps. Eva Braun looked in the crystal
mirror at her cunt. Which size

did your thighs have, Eva Braun? I know girls
who look exactly like the Eva Braun who looks
like Eva Braun in the photo. I grew
up, considered my pubic hairs, considered

nipples, considered the reeds, years
later I considered the picture of Eva Braun.
In the same month a breast of the
wife of the American president would be

geschnitten, auf einem anderen historischen
Foto wetzen alte Herren ihre Arschlöcher
nach der Konferenz auf den brokatbespannten
Sesseln, der südliche Vormittag ist voller

Schrott, Staub, zerfallender Konstruktionen. Was war
mit den Darmwürmern, die Adolf Hitlers Schäfer
Hund hatte? Was war mit Eva Braun? Eine
Lesebuchgeschichte, die man erzwang wie

Jahre darauf die Interpretationen, endete.
Halb Österreich reiste mit einem Zug an,
küßte Eva Braun die Hand, sah nach den Titten,
plombiert durch Dauerwellen. Adolf Hitler

verteilte Postkarten. Ich sah meine
Mutter auf einem Foto in einer langen Reihe
sitzen und lachen, ich sah meinen Vater
eine Chaussee auf einem Foto entlang

gehen, naiv in Uniform wie ein Chausseebaum,
was spielten sie, als sie fotografiert
wurden? Ich sah die Bügelfalten in der Hose
Adolf Hitlers auf einem Foto, ich sah mit vier

Jahren einen dunklen Bahnhof vorüber
gleiten 1944, ich sah ein emailliertes Schild
mit blauer und gelber Wolle und Stricknadeln
an der roten Backsteinwand eines Bahnhofs,

Eva Braun, hat Adolf Hitler deine Möhse
mit der Zunge zärtlich gestreichelt? Adolf
Hitler, hat Eva Braun deinen Schwanz zärtlich
gelutscht? Oder war das tabuisiert durch

Staat und Politik? Wichsflecken an dem Winter
Mantel, ein paar Generäle auf dem Abtritt,
sie zeichneten Schlachtpläne auf die Scheiß
Hauswand, nannten Namen, Höhen, Einsätze,

cut off, in another historical
photo old men polished their assholes
on brocade-lined armchairs after
the conference, the southern afternoon is full of

junk, dust, crumbling constructions. What was
with the intestinal worms which Adolf Hitler's German
shepherd had? What was with Eva Braun? A
storybook story which one suppressed

like years later the interpretations, ended.
Half of Austria arrived in a train,
kissed Eva Braun's hand, looked at her tits,
sealed with permanent waves. Adolf Hitler

passed out postcards. I saw my
mother in a photo in a long row
sitting and laughing, I saw my father
in a photo going along a tree-lined avenue,

naive in uniform like an avenue tree,
what were they playing as they were
photographed? I saw the creases in the pants
of Adolf Hitler in a photo, I saw, four years

old, a dark train station passing
by in 1944, I saw an enameled sign
with blue and yellow wool and knitting needles
on the red brick wall of a train station,

Eva Braun, did Adolf Hitler tenderly stroke
your pussy with his tongue? Adolf
Hitler, did Eva tenderly suck your
cock? Or was that taboo thanks to

the state and politics? Come stains on the winter
coat, a couple of generals in the toilet,
they drew battle plans on the shitty
wall, named names, heights, deployments,

Eva Braun, was hast du gespürt, als du die
Kapsel kriegtest? Hast du einfach gedacht,
verpaßt? Hast du gedacht, jetzt hab ichs ver
paßt gekriegt? Und die Zähne des Schäferhunds

fielen nach der starken Injektion aus dem Kiefer.
Der Orgasmus des Todes ist billiger als der
Orgasmus des Lebens, wobei fraglich ist, ob
der Orgasmus des Todes nicht einfach gestautes

Leben ist, das explodiert. Warum ist das
Leben in den vielen nicht jeden Tag?
Warum Dauerwellen, Eva Braun?
Warum lächelst du, Eva Braun? Warum

nimmst du Hustensaft, Eva Braun? Hat Adolf
Hitler nicht gewußt, das die österreichische
Psychoanalyse, liegt in den Sätzen, lügt? Nie
bin ich an dem Flüßchen Inn gewesen, habe

auch keine Lust, auf das Wasser zu schauen,
habe auch keine Lust, auf das Wasser in Köln
zu schauen, totes Wasser, voll toter Fische und
Pflanzen, totes Wasser, worum sie kämpften, Grenzen,

Kohlen, Feuer für die Industrie, Stahltürme, Glut
in der Nacht, tanzende Gestalten vor dem offenen
Feuer der Industrieanlagen, kein Heiliger schwimmt
in diesen toten Wassern, kein Heiliger spuckt

aus dem Apartmentfenster, kruder ist besser
dadurchzugehen als Pillen zu nehmen, die Patente,
Eva Braun, wie war das für dich unter der Dusche,
Deutsche Holzkohle, Flamingoblumen, Schwertlilien

und Kübel? Adolf Hitler im Nachthemd,
im Beton, unter der Erdoberfläche,
Flitter der Nerven, über die Akten
tanzend, er träumte irre im Betonbunker,

Eva Braun, what did you feel when you
got the capsule? Did you simply think
you'd had your chance? Did you think,
now I've had it? And the teeth of the German shepherd

fell out of his jaw after the strong injection.
The orgasm of death is cheaper than the
orgasm of life, although it's questionable whether
the orgasm of death isn't simply pent up

life that explodes. Why isn't life
in the multitudes every day?
Why permanent waves, Eva Braun?
Why are you smiling, Eva Braun? Why

do you take cough syrup, Eva Braun? Didn't Adolf
Hitler know that the Austrian
psychoanalysis, lying in the sentences, lies? I
was never at the river Inn, also

have no desire to look at the water,
also have no desire to look at the water in Cologne,
dead water, full of dead fish and
plants, dead water, which they fought over, borders,

coals, fires for the industry, furnaces, embers
in the night, dancing figures before the open
fires of the industrial complexes, no holy saint swims
in these dead waters, no holy saint spits

out the apartment window, the crude passing through
is better than taking pills, the patents,
Eva Braun, how was it for you under the shower,
German charcoal, flamingo flowers, Spanish irises

and pails? Adolf Hitler in a nightshirt,
in the cement, under the earth's surface,
sparkle of nerves, dancing over the
files, he dreamed madly in the cement bunker,

hat vermutlich niemanden persönlich
geschlagen, er hatte genug andere, die für
ihn schlugen, immer sind da andere, die unter
zeichnen, schlagen, hängen, immer sind da tat

sächlich andere, Angestellte, Sekretärinnen,
Aktenboten, Wahnsinn, Eva Braun, du Strohpuppe,
Rauch, Zyankali, Spurenelemente, Unterschriften,
die plötzlich lebendig werden und dann einzelne

Personen sind, Dinge, die schäbigen Dinge, sie
stehen im Raum. Stand Adolf Hitler mit steifem
Schwanz vor dir im Raum, Eva Braun? Wer hat deine
Büstenhalter gewaschen, Eva Braun? Hast du an

Persil gedacht? Die Weltgeschichte in Form der
Industriecomics, Eva Braun, Spitzenkleid im
großen Saal, unter den Menschenstimmen, hoch
gezogene Schulter, hast du sie gesehen? Was ist

mit den gefärbten Haaren? Was ist mit dem Alt
Hochdeutschen? Was ist mit den versteinerten
Liebesgeschichten? Wortgespenster, Dreckskerle
der Geschichte, die durch die Reime irren,

zwischen den Filmschatten Berlins, Schatten
Gebärden, Leinwandschatten, Schattenschreie,
zusammenstürzende Schatten, später mit einer
Tonspur unterlegt, nachsynchronisierte

Lippenbewegungen, Eva Braun, in welchen Illu
Strierten hast du gelesen? Ich muß mich erinnern:
meine Mutter liebte Flugzeuge und Gespenster,
die wiedererschienen, Phantome, sie träumte davon,

noch bevor sie für die Männer des Flugplatzes
kochte, in ihrem seltsamen Französisch, mein
Vater mit seinem Schulenglisch lieh sich
einen Wagen, das Verdeck runtergeklappt, sie

supposedly never hit anyone
personally, he had others enough to do
his hitting, there are always others who
sign, hit, hang, indeed there are

always others, employees, secretaries,
office boys, insanity, Eva Braun, you straw puppet,
smoke, cyanide, trace elements, signatures,
which suddenly become single living

persons, things, the shabby things, they're
standing in the room. Did Adolf Hitler stand before you
in the room with a stiff cock, Eva Braun? Who washed
your bra, Eva Braun? Did you think about

Persil laundry soap? World history in the form of
industrial comics, Eva Braun, a lace dress in the
large hall, among the human voices, shoulders
lifted high, did you see them? What's with

the dyed hair? What's with that old high
German? What's with the fossilized
love stories? Word-ghosts, dirty bastards
of history, stumbling through the rhymes,

between the film-shadows of Berlin, shadow
gestures, projection-screen-shadows, shadow-screams,
collapsing shadows, later accompanied
by a soundtrack, synchronized

lip movements, Eva Braun, in which
magazines were you reading? I have to remember:
my mother loved airplanes and ghosts,
which reappeared, phantoms, she dreamed of them,

even before she cooked for the men at the
airfield, in her odd French, my
father borrowed a car in his school-English,
the top rolled back, they

hielten in der Landschaft, sie fickten an
einem warmen gelben Kornfeldrand im Juli.
Meine Mutter liebte Groschenromane, sie sah
nach, ob die Strumpfnaht gerade saß, sie ging

in einem seidigen Glimmerkleid über die Wiese.
Der Schwiegervater vermachte seine Bibliothek dem
Staat Israel aus einem sentimentalen Grund,
und was ist vorher geschehen, daß diese Formen

entstanden, sentimentaler als die Erinnerung
an Hausecken und Straßennamen? Sentimentaler
als Dauerwellen auf einem Foto? Ich muß mich
erinnern an die bleiche Vorortsiedlung, ich

muß mich erinnern an den Lastwagen, der
plötzlich vor dem Haus hielt, vollgepackt mit
Menschen und Hausrat, Einquartierungen, die
Fremdheit noch fremder zu machen, abgehakt von

den Listen, Henkeltöpfe, Aktentaschen, Pomade
Scheitel, die nichts hatten, besaßen den Wahn
Sinn nie besessener imaginärer Güter, wenn sie
sprachen, woher sie kamen, die Biografien versaut

durch das tote Österreich, alte Mythen, Brachacker,
der Gegensatz ist nicht die Industrie, der Gegen
Satz verschwindet auf den alten Fotos, in denen
die Geschichte ringsum zerfiel, Eva Braun, Milch

Glasfenster, Portale, Koma in einem schwedischen
Hotelzimmer, Spritzen ins Bein überm Socken
Halter. Nun werfen die Rechenmaschinen Knochen
in die Luft, Stanley Kubrick, der Filmtrick ist

durchschaut trotz vier Kanalstereogeräuschen im
roten Plüschkino Sohos, wo ich eines regnerischen
Abends bin, allein durch London gehend, still,
zusammengefaßt in dem hellgrauen, windigen

stopped in the countryside, they fucked
at the edge of a warm yellow wheat field in July.
My mother loved cheap paperbacks, she looked
to see if the seam in her stockings was straight, she went

across the meadow in a silky shimmering dress.
The father-in-law left his library to the
state of Israel for a sentimental reason,
and what happened before, that these forms

developed, more sentimental than the memory
of house-corners and street names? More sentimental
than permanent waves in a photo? I have to
remember the pale suburban settlement, I

have to think about the truck that
suddenly stopped in front of the house, packed with
people and their belongings, billets to make
the foreignness even foreigner, checked off

the lists, bedpans, briefcases, pomaded and
parted, they had nothing, owned the in-
sanity of never-owned imaginary goods, if they
spoke, from where they came, the biographies ruined

by dead Austria, old myths, fallow fields,
the opposite is not the industry, the oppo-
site disappears in the old photos, in which
history disintegrated all around, Eva Braun, opaque

window glass, portals, coma in a Swedish
hotel room, shots in the leg above the stocking
garter. Now the computers are tossing bones
in the air, Stanley Kubrick, the film trick

is revealed, despite four-channel-stereo in
the red-plush cinemas of Soho, where I am one
rainy evening, walking through London alone, quiet,
collected, in the light gray, windy

Februarabend, zerfallenes London, elegische
Westendstraßen, elegische Reklamen, elegische
Theatergebäude und Stripteaseclubs, elegische
dreckige Buchläden im abgelagerten

trüben Staub, tropfende kaputte Wasserrohre an
den Hausfronten, ein sinnloses Alarmklingelgeräusch
an einer Hauswand, gelber verdüsterter Anstrich,
Hauseingänge mit den Namen von Körperfleisch,

sie sind für einige Augenblicke zu kaufen,
Berührungen von einsamem Schwanz und
kalter Fotze vor der dünnen Gasheizung des
Mietzimmers, trostlos in den Gestrüppen der

Zahlen verirrt, trostlos im Geld eingefroren.
Eva Braun, wer hat dir Postkarten geschrieben?
Eva Braun, hast du jemals frierend am Piccadilly
gestanden? Eva Braun, was sagtest du in dem Moment,

als das Foto gemacht wurde? Nach dem Film krieche
ich fröstelnd unter die dünne Decke eines billigen
Hotels in Bayswater, Haltestelle Odeon, das Monster
Viertel Londons, zerfallene Hinterhöfe, verscharrte

Körper, der gasbeheizte Kamin wärmt nicht, die
Zimmertapete ist fleckig, ich lese noch ein
Gedicht von Frank O'Hara und W. C. Williams, ich
trinke den Rest kalt gewordenen Kaffees aus dem

Pappbecher, der auf dem Marmor über dem Kamin
steht, ich bin allein in diesen amerikanischen
Gedichten und schaue mich darin um inmitten dieser
Londonnacht, gelbe Nebelbeleuchtung an den Straßen

Rändern, victorianische Monstersäulen und Portale
die ganze Straße entlang, Fenster mit Pappe davor,
Gardinenfetzen, und plötzlich, in der Stille, total
irrsinnig, erinnere ich mich an das Pausenzeichen

February evening, decaying London, elegiac
West End streets, elegiac advertisements, elegiac
theater buildings and striptease clubs, elegiac
filthy book stores under aged,

murky dust, rusted leaky water pipes along
the house fronts, a senselessly ringing alarm
on a house wall, dismally yellowed paint,
entrances with the names of bodily flesh,

which for a few moments can be bought,
contact between a lonely cock and
a cold cunt before the weak gas heater of
the rented room, miserable and lost in the

maze of numbers, bleak and frozen in the money.
Eva Braun, who wrote you postcards?
Eva Braun, have you ever stood freezing in
Piccadilly? Eva Braun, what did you say in the moment

when that photo was taken? After the movie I crawl
shivering under the thin blanket of a cheap
hotel in Bayswater, Odeon station, the monster
quarter of London, crumbling courtyards, buried

bodies, the gas-fired fireplace doesn't heat, the
wallpaper is stained, I read a few more
poems by Frank O'Hara and W.C. Williams, I
drink the rest of some cold coffee out of

the paper cup that stands on the marble mantle
over the fireplace, I'm alone in these American
poems and see myself in them in the middle of this
London night, yellow fog lights along the

streets, Victorian monster-columns and portals
the whole street long, windows patched with cardboard,
curtain-scraps, and suddenly, in the silence, completely
crazy, I remember the call sign

der BBC im Radio eines Morgens im Krieg. Ich
erinnere mich an die Nachkriegsschokolade der
englischen Soldaten, blaue Pflaumen auf einem
Karren, der durch die Hinterhöfe geschoben wurde,

Straußwalzer, einen dunklen Kinoraum und Krieg.
Ein Knochen, in die Luft geworfen, ein Totschläger
Werkzeug auf der weißen Leinwand des Gedächtnisses,
ein flimmernder Schatten, hinter Zierblumen versteckt,

ist mit den Schattengeräuschen aus dem Stereokanal
nichts als ein Schatten im gespenstischen, wahnsinnigen
Ballsaal des Todes, der die Luft ist, der Tod wirft
Blasen in die Luft, viel besser ist friedlich aus

zuruhen und ein Leberwurstbrötchen zu essen in
der Mittagspause, besser ist die Pflaumen aus dem
Kühlschrank aufzuessen ohne sich zu entschuldigen,
besser ist den Rest Kaffee aus dem Pappbecher

auszutrinken in dem Hotelzimmer nachts, besser als
Filmaufnahmen, Luftaufnahmen, Eva Braun, denke ich
hier in dieser Kölner Nacht, stickig und düster,
während ich auf ein Foto schaue, das die Liebes

Geschichte, kitschig und nachcoloriert,
erzählt, Eva Braun, kleines Monstrum in
der Dekoration, das blöde und traurig lächelt
auf dem Foto, und ehe das Foto gemacht wurde,

wirklich. Die Augenbrauen sind
nachgezeichnet, du hast den Mund geöffnet, die Lippen
sind geschminkt, sitzt die Strumpfnaht? Trägst du
ein Blümchenkleid? Hat jemand deine Frisur in

Unordnung gebracht? Was ist mit dem Akzent? Hat
jemand dich geil angeschaut, dein etwas fettes Baby
Gesicht? Hast du deine Fotze vergessen? Trocknete
deine Fotze vor Schreck ein, als der Krieg begann?

of the BBC radio one morning during the war. I
remember the after-the-war-chocolate of
the English soldiers, blue plums on a
cart, which was being pushed through a courtyard,

Strauss waltzes, a dark movie theater and war.
A bone tossed in the air, a killer's
tool on the white screen of the memory,
a flickering shadow, hidden behind ornamental flowers,

together with the shadow-noises from the stereo speakers
is nothing but a shadow in the eerie, insane
ballroom of Death, which is the air, Death blows
bubbles in the air, it's much better to relax

peacefully with a liverwurst sandwich during
the lunch break, better to eat the plums out
of the icebox without saying you're sorry,
better to drink cold coffee from a paper cup

in a hotel room at night, better than
moving pictures, aerial photographs, Eva Braun, I'm
thinking here in this Cologne night, stuffy and dismal,
while I look at a photo, which tells of the love

story, kitschy and hand-colored,
Eva Braun, little monster among
the decor, smiling stupid and sad
in the photo, and before the photo was taken,

really. The eyebrows are
touched up, your mouth is open, lipstick
on the lips, are the stocking seams straight? Are you
wearing a flowered dress? Has someone

messed up your hair? What's with the accent? Did
someone give you a horny look, your slightly fat baby
face? Have you forgotten your cunt? Did your
cunt dry up out of fear as the war began?

Berliner Himmel, als ich mit einer Panam-Maschine
einflog, sah ich zuerst einen Friedhof zwischen
den Häusern, die Herren legten ihre
Tageszeitungen auf die leeren Sitze,

der Taxifahrer fluchte über die Passanten, als
die Lichter erschienen. Im Ubahnschacht hielt je
mand sein blutiges, tropfendes Gesicht zwischen
den Händen und drehte sich zur Fliesenwand,

als die automatischen Türen sich
schlossen. Hast du mit Gütermann's Nähseide
Strümpfe gestopft? Wie hast du im Badeanzug aus
gesehen? Hast du dir die Achselhöhlen ausrasiert?

Ausrasierte Achselhöhlen sehen immer nach Seife
und Deodoranten aus, stoppelig und glatt.
Die Fantasie hat die Industrie über
nommen mit ihren Angestellten.

Hast du ein Leberwurstbrötchen
gegessen? Hat dir das Leberwurstbrötchen geschmeckt?
Hatte Adolf Hitler Schweißfüße? Küßte er deine Hand?
Redete er im Schlaf? Was hast du

gegen Kopfschmerzen genommen? Was hast du
gedacht, als du den Kurfürstendamm entlangchauffiert
wurdest? Im verblassenden Schatten morgens 5 Uhr
sitze ich dort zwischen den zusammengestellten,

abgeschlossenen Sommerstühlen und Tischen, rauche
Kiff im Schatten von Café Kranzler-Markisen und gehe
durch die Tränengasnebel und Glasscherben der zer
trümmerten großen Schaufensterscheiben, die Nutten

haben sich schnell verzogen, als vor einigen Stunden
der Straßenkrieg losging, dann fahre ich mit der ersten
Stadtbahn zum Wannsee, wo ein paar Schwäne zwischen
dem Abfall am Ufer schaukeln, ein toter Landungssteg,

Berlin sky, as I flew in with a Pan Am plane,
I first saw a cemetery between
the houses, the gentlemen laid their
newspapers on the empty seats,

the taxi driver swore about the passers-by as
the lights went on. In the subway hall
someone held their bloody, dripping face between
their hands and turned toward the tiled wall

as the automatic doors slammed
shut. Did you mend your stockings with
Güterman's silk thread? How did you look in
a swimsuit? Did you shave your armpits?

Shaved armpits always look like soap
and deodorant, stubbly and slick.
Fantasy has taken over the industry
with its employees.

Did you eat a liverwurst
sandwich? Did the liverwurst sandwich taste good?
Did Adolf Hitler have sweaty feet? Did he kiss your hand?
Did he talk in his sleep? What did you take

against the headaches? What did you think
as you were chauffeured along the Kurfürstendamm?
In the fading shadows of 5 in the morning
I sit there between the folded up,

locked up patio chairs and tables, smoke
kif in the shadow of the Café Kranzler awning and walk
through the tear gas clouds and shards of glass
from the shattered storefront windows, the whores

having hastily retreated as the street battle began
a few hours ago, then I take the first subway
train to the Wannsee, where a couple of swans are rocking
between the garbage along the shore, a lifeless pier,

eine dünne Morgendämmerung, hellgrau. Was für
eine Pelzjacke hast du getragen? Was für eine Zahnpaste
benutzt? Ich zittere in der Morgendämmerung in
Berlin, nehme die Socken von der Heizungsröhre,

lasse die Verdunklung runter. Es ist schade,
daß du nicht die Liebe erfunden hast, Eva Braun.
Ich schreibe dieses Rock'n'Roll Lied über euren
furchtbaren Wahnsinn, Eva Braun. Hätte dir dieses

Lied gefallen? Hättest du beim Tanzen geschwitzt?
Was habt ihr geredet, als ihr allein im Betonbunker
wart? Warum die Farbe Braun? Was hat die Zunge verlangt?
Keiner hat Adolf Hitler geliebt, und er mußte deswegen

den Krieg gewinnen? Hast du die Körper gesehen? Hast
du die Nahkampfspangen gesehen? Hast du die Flammen
Werfer gesehen? Hast du die verbrannten Gesichter
gesehen? Hast du die Gaskrüppel gesehen? Hast du

die Todesvirenkultur gesehen? Hast du die
Blumenschatten gesehen? Hast
du aus dem Fenster geschaut? Hast du die Nacht
Tischlampe ausgeknipst? Die Dauerwellen der

Ordnung auf deinem Kopf, deine fette, bloße
Schulter, deine Unterhosen vom Kaufhaus, dein
durchgeknipstes Ohrläppchen für den Stein, dein
Taschentuch mit dem Nasenschleim, das Camelia

zwischen den Beinen, deine Arschrundungen in dem
Hüftgürtel, deine Brustwarzen, blieben sie ein
Geheimnis? Inmitten der historischen Kriegsschau
Plätze, der Krieg ist ein Schauplatz, wer schaut

da zu? Ist eine Liebesgeschichte nötig, die so
viele Fragen braucht? Nun bist du in dem historischen
Foto verschwunden. Nun gehen die Verkleidungen
herum. Nun ist die Geschichte zusammengebrochen und aus.

a weak dawn, light gray. What kind of
fur coat did you wear? What kind of toothpaste
did you use? I tremble in the first dawn in
Berlin, take the socks from the radiator,

let down the shades. It's a pity
that you didn't invent love, Eva Braun.
I write this rock 'n' roll song about your
terrible insanity, Eva Braun. Would you have

liked this song? Would you have sweated as you danced?
What did you talk about as you were alone in the cement
bunker? Why the color brown? What did the tongue demand?
No one loved Adolf Hitler, and that was why he

had to win the war? Did you see the bodies?
Did you see the hand-to-hand combat? Did you see the
flame-throwers? Did you see the burned faces?
Did you see the gas-cripples? Did you

see the killer-virus spores? Did you see the
flower-shadows? Did you
look out the window? Did you turn off the
nightstand lamp? The permanent waves of

order on your head, your fat, bare
shoulder, your underwear from the department store,
your pierced ear lobe for the jewel, your
handkerchief with the mucous, the camellia

between the legs, your ass-shapes in the
garter belt, your nipples, will they remain a
secret? In the middle of the historical showplaces
of the war, the war is a showplace, who even

looks? Is a love story necessary that needs
so many questions? Now you've disappeared in the
historical photo. Now the disguises are going
around. Now the story is broken down and over.

4. (D-Zug)

: aus dem heruntergezogenen
Fenster das Zeitungspapier wehen
lassen, eine Kinderhand, mit dem

Papierfetzen daran,

das Elend (Ausland), das in diesem Land
investiert, sitz an jeder
flüchtig erblickten

Straßenecke, traurige, müde Gesichter,
ohne Ausdruck, Tränensäcke, Falten um den
eingezogenen Mund,

eine junge Frau weint vor Erschöpfung
in einer zweieinhalb Zimmerwohnung, in der
aufgefalteten Architektur der Geometrie,
es ist nachts und die Heizungsröhren knacken,

Zitat: „das gefährlichste Tier, das existiert, ist
der Architekt. Er hat mehr verwüstet als der Krieg."

Haarausfall nach der Geburt, Erschrecken
auf der Straße, mitten am Tag, wenn man stehen
bleibt, umgeben von den vielen, die abwesend

blicken, aufwachen, husten & in den

Ausguß spucken, verschobene Materialverhältnisse,
die zarten Körper an die Hauswände gedrückt durch
die Wagen, alle dieselben Reihen von den Vorort

Straßen bis in die Innenstadt,

laufende, einzelne Körper zwischen den

Kolonnen der Autoindustrie, verwischte Gestalten

4. (D-Train)

: letting the newspaper
flutter out the rolled down window,
a child's hand, with the

shreds of paper against it,

the misery (foreign countries), which invests in this
country, sits on every
furtively glanced-at

street corner, sad, tired faces,
without expression, bags under the eyes, lines around
the tight-lipped mouth,

a young woman cries from exhaustion
in a two-and-a-half room apartment, in the
unfolded architecture of geometry,
it's night and the heating pipes are ticking,

Quote: "The most dangerous animal that exists is
the architect. He has destroyed more than the war."

Hair loss following birth, fear
on the street, in the middle of the day, if one stands
still, surrounded by the multitudes, the absent

glances, waking up, coughing & spitting

in the sink, postponed material circumstances,
the delicate bodies pushed up against the walls by
the cars, the same rows of suburban streets

all the way into the inner city,

single, running bodies between the

convoys of the auto industry, blurred figures

hinter dreckbespritzen Securitglasfenstern, kleiner
als ihre eigenen Körper in den Industriegehäusen,

das Zeitungspapier zerreißt im Fahrtwind,

Papierfetzen treiben über die engen Gärten am
Bahndamm, Drachen aus stinkiger
Druckerschwärze, Collagen des
alltäglichen langsamen Irrsinns,

erstarrter Wirbel aus Wörtern: Handelsnamen,

Reptiliengehirn, Haß, Verleumdungen, Semantik, die

großen Familien machen weiter. In den Straßen
die abgemagerten Mädchenkörper, Knochen mit etwas
Haut darüber, in bunten Lumpen von Second-Hand-Läden,

„when the music's over" zwischen den regen

verwaschenen alten Reklamebildern, (Neonlicht
erloschene Neugier zu leben, Kalligrafien)

erloschene Poesie. Die Morgendämmerungen

sind feucht und undurchdringlich, Massen geduckter
Gestalten, sie verschwinden in den Büros, sie gehen
in die Läden, sie müssen in Schulen, Kindergärten,

ihre Lebensformen ausgeprägt zwischen

Warenreihen und Regalen, im Pestlichtgeflacker des TV
erscheinen abends die Gesichter der Politiker und
diskutieren, im Pestlichtgeflacker des

TV erscheinen die fremden Geschichten
an der Zimmerwand: erinnerst du dich

„until the end" an die dunklen Hauseingänge,
in denen wir zusammenstanden,

behind the dirt-flecked security glass windows, smaller
than their own bodies in the industrial shells,

the newspaper rips in the headwind,

shreds of paper drift over the narrow gardens
along the tracks, kites made of stinky
printer's ink, collages of the
daily gradual madness,

frozen swirls of words: brand names,

reptile brains, hate, slander, semantics, the

big families continue on. In the streets
the skinny girls' bodies, bones with a little
skin over them, in colorful rags from the second-hand store,

"when the music's over" between the rain-

faded old advertisements, (neon-light
extinguished curiosity to live, calligraphy)

extinguished poetry. The dawns

are damp and impassable, masses of bent-over
figures, they disappear in the offices, they go
into the stores, they have to go to schools, kindergartens,

their ways of life distinctive between

rows of products and shelves, in the pestilent-light-flicker
of the TV at night the faces of the politicians appear
and discuss, in the pestilent-light-flicker

of the TV the strange faces appear
on the wall of the room: do you remember

"until the end" the dark house entrances,
in which we stood together,

erinnerst du dich an deine eigenen Küsse in dem
Treppenhaus, erinnerst du dich überhaupt noch an

Küsse? (Oder was

du fühltest?) Eingetaucht in das leuchtende Gras
an den Wegrändern, vom offenen Zugfenster aus gesehen,
lassen wir die Zeitungsfetzen fliegen.

Gelbes Nachmittagslicht spiegelt sich in den Fenstern
an denen wir vorbeifahren, Septembergelb

und was ist das für ein Land,

was für Gedanken sind hier

zu Ende gedacht, endgültig zu Ende,

zu Ende, „die Aristokratie

der Gefühle," hahahaha, das ist

nicht mein Geschmack,

falls überhaupt einer damit was zu tun hatte,
IBM-Schreibmaschinengefühle und Küsse,

Ich strecke meine Füße aus,
übereinandergeschlagen, in diesem
Abteil, die weißen Converse All

wie paßt das
zusammen?

Star Basketballschue, 12 Dollar
auf dem roten Kunststoffsitz, und noch einmal das
Stück Zeitung zerrissen für das Kind am offenen

Zugfenster: wie die Wörter fliegen (Masken),

die Fetzen, es ist ein sanfter Nachmittag wie
selten, Licht über den bleichen, monotonen
Städten, sanftes Nachmittagslicht

do you remember your own kisses in the
stairwell, do you remember kisses

at all? (Or what

you felt?) Submerged in the glowing grass
along the paths, seen from the open train window,
we let the newspaper shreds fly.

Yellow afternoon light reflects in the windows
which we pass by, September-yellow

and what kind of country is this,

what kind of thoughts are

thought to the finish here, finally to the end,

the end "the aristocracy

of feelings," hahahaha, that's

not to my taste,

if anyone should have anything to do with that at all,
IBM-typewriter-feelings and kisses,

I stretch out my feet,
one over the other, in this
compartment, the white Converse All

how does that
fit together?

Star basketball shoes, 12 dollars,
on the red plastic seat, and once again the
piece of newspaper torn for the child at the open

train window: how the words fly (masks),

the fragments, it's one of those gentle afternoons that
we rarely have, light over the pale, monotone
cities, soft afternoon light

auf die bröckeligen Fassaden der Vorstädte

und Reihenhäuser, sanftes Septembernachmittagslicht

auf den Gesichtern an den offenen Fenstern, an
denen wir vorüberfahren,
sanfte Menschengesichter
im September,

der Haß der Zeitungen zerreißt, flattert als
Papier in der Hand, das fröhliche
Geräusch im fahrenden

D-Zug: der uns aus den nordwestlichen
Gebieten Westdeutschlands durch die
Zone der Industrie und Profite

bringt, stehengelassene tote Fördertürme, schwarze
Räder in der Luft,
Schlackenhalden,
tote Wege, schwarze, verkohlte
Dampflokomotiven auf einem toten

Gleis, verrostende Schienenspuren

& abgestorbener Ginster am Bahndamm, erinnerst du
dich wirklich an deine eigenen Küsse?

Und wenn die Industrie
Westdeutschlands
zusammenbricht?

(„Oh hier raus sein,
Hier wo alles nach Wunsch
eintraf bis auf das Neue")

„Hier in diesem Land lebe ich!": lebst du
wirklich?

Nein, nicht diese
Empfindung.

(„Weitab und
im fremden Land
sein." E. P.)

Hier ist bis jetzt nur Ausland gewesen, worauf du
schaust,

on the crumbling facades of the suburbs

and tract homes, soft September-afternoon-light

on the faces in the open windows
which we pass by,
gentle human-faces
in September,

the hate of the newspapers rips, flutters as
paper in the hand, that cheerful
sound in the moving

D-Train: it brings us from the northwest
regions of West Germany through the
zones of industry and profit,

dead, abandoned winding-towers, black
wheels in the air,
slag heaps,
dead roads, black, sooty
steam locomotives on a dead

track, rusted railway lines

& dust-coated Scotch broom along the embankment, do you
really remember your own kisses?

And when the West
German industry
collapses?

("Oh to be out of here,
here where everything went
as wished except for the new")

"Here in this land I live!": do you really
live?

No, not this
sensation.

("To be far away
and in a foreign
country." E.P.)

Until now this was a foreign country, wherever you
look,

der Kastanien
Baum in dem
lichtlosen
engen Hof,

stillstehende
Aufzüge,

das Kalender
Monatsbild
an einer
Bürowand,

Sonnen
Blenden,

Erinnerung: ich höre die zittrige
Stimme des Dichters auf einer Schall
Platte in einem Apartment, unheimliche
Korridore abends
und ohne Stimmen, vielleicht 60 Namen
auf der Namenstafel am Ein
Gang vor der Glastür, früh abgeschlos-
sen, das Treppenhaus erlischt, ein roter
Leuchtknopf am Ende des Ganges, und dann
inmitten der Leblosigkeit hinter ei
ner Tür Fernsehfilmgeräusche, als
ich dort entlanggehe/die Stimme des
Dichters eines Sonntag
Vormittags hingestottert, und
jetzt, nach den Korridoren, in diesem
Westdeutschen Apartment Jahre danach
wieder plötzlich)

Liegende Venus und CocaCola 1974,
Verben in einer durchgehenden Chronologie,
„dieses CocaCola der ganzen Welt“

warum willst du schön sprechen?

„Müssen wir Idioten sein und träumen in den
Halbobscuritäten einer zwielichtigen Stimmung,
um Dichter zu sein?“
(W. C. W.)

Abgebrannt in einem schönen Septemberlicht, die
persönliche Ökonomie: ein totales Disaster,

ist die Ökonomie ein persönliches Gefühl? Widersprüche
weil ich spreche, Widersprüche weil ich daran

denke: Notizen, am Zeitungsrand, der zerfetzt wird. Die
wenigen Freunde über die Vororte
verstreut, die neuen Freunde einzeln über die Länder

verteilt

Verschiedene
Stimmen,

<table>
<tr><td></td><td>Memory: I hear the shaky</td></tr>
<tr><td>The chestnut
tree in the
lightless
narrow courtyard,</td><td>voice of the poet on a record
in an apartment, evening,
sinister hallways
and without voices, maybe 60 names
on the nameplate in the entryway</td></tr>
<tr><td>still-standing
elevators,</td><td>by the glass door, locked early,
the stairwell light out, a red
glowing light switch at the end of the hall,</td></tr>
<tr><td>the calendar
picture
on a
office wall,</td><td>and then in the midst of the lifelessness
television film sounds behind a door
as I walk along there / the voice of the
poet stuttering in on a
Sunday morning, and</td></tr>
<tr><td>sun
blinds,</td><td>now, after the hallways, in this
West German apartment years later
suddenly again)</td></tr>
</table>

Prone Venus and Coca Cola 1974,
verbs in a continuous chronology,
"this Coca Cola of the entire world"

why do you want to speak nicely?

"Must we be idiots and dream in the
partial obscurities of a dubious mood
in order to be poets?"
(W.C.W.)

Burned out in a beautiful September light, the
personal economy: a total disaster,

is the economy a personal feeling? Contradictions
because I speak, contradictions because I think

about it: notes in the newspaper margin, being torn to
shreds. The few friends scattered about the
suburbs, the new friends strewn singly across the country-

side. Different
voices,

verschiedene Biografien,

Abweichungen, „gut so.“

Diskussion: Wo alles auf einen Zusammenhang drängt...

Was hast du gespürt,
als du mit deinen Lippen über den
nackten Körper getastet hast, was hast du

inmitten der zerschundenen Landschaft

gespürt, Wortgötter,
Seitenstraßensex,
unter den arrangierten Maschinen?
Laß mich
erinnern, sagst du,
laß mich erinnern, laß mich

allein, sagst du, laß mich, sanftes Gesicht

im sanften Septemberlicht,
wie jetzt: antworte sanft

antworte, „inmitten der täglichen
Ausräuberungen, wie?“

Wie die Gesichter in den offenen Nachmittagsfenstern
antworte nicht. Da ist ein blechernes Feld, zerbeult,

„valse d'autumn“ oder wie so'n Gefühl heißt, nicht,

die Klarheit beim Rausschauen aus einem D-Zugfenster,
sanft, sanfter Rhythmus jetzt hier,

laß mich, laß mich erinnern, sagst du.
Kleine Bahnhöfe tauchen auf und bleiben zurück,

unbedeutende Gebilde, : bleiben zurück?
unbedeutende Haltepunkte : unbedeutende?

different biographies,

deviations, "good so."

Discussion: Where everything is forced to connect...

What did you feel
as you touched the naked body
with your lips, what did you

feel in the middle of the trashed

landscape, word-gods,
side-street-sex,
under the arranged machines?

Let me
remember, you say,
let me remember, leave me

alone, you say, leave me, gentle face

in a soft September light,
like now: answer softly

answer, "in the midst of the daily
plundering, or?"

Like the faces in the open afternoon-windows
don't answer. There is a sheet-metal field, dented,

"valse d'autumn" or how such a feeling is called,

not the clarity of looking out a D-Train window,
gentle, gentle rhythm here now,

let me, let me remember, you say.
Small train stations appear and remain behind,

meaningless structures, : remain behind?
meaningless stops : meaningless?

gelbrote Feuer
auf einem Schrottplatz,

sanft, sanftes Gehölz, kleine Reste von
Wäldern, in denen noch die dünnen Morgen
Nebel hängen, Spuren von Nässe, nicht

umgeknickt, kleine friedliche Tümpel, vergessen

am Rand eines Besitztums (:„wir kommen zurück,“
in das Haus, wir kehren heim, Heim?) für die
Augen eine flüchtige Rast, aus dem Zugfenster

schauend, der lange, langsame

gleichmäßige Blick über dieses Land. Da ist
Geducktes Grün, fantastisches Grün, das vorüberzieht,
und eine Kinderhand ist aus dem Zugfenster

gestreckt.

Warum Traurigkeiten? All: Ihr sanften

Gesichter im Nachmittagslicht, (keine Gesichter
: ihr sanften Gesichter zwischen für die Münzen)
den Reklamewänden, ihr sanften

Gesichter in den Fensterrahmen,

ihr sanften Gesichter im Septemberlicht, ihr
sanften Gesichter Westdeutschlands, müde und traurig,
ihr sanften Gesichter, hungrig nach Fotze, Schwanz,
Titten, hungrig nach einer Exotik alltäglichen

Lebens, hungrig nach einem Kuß, hungrig
euren eigenen Kuß zwischen den Wänden zu spüren,

hungrig zwischen den Reklamen, hungrig zwischen
den Anzeigen, hungrig zwischen den Bildern,

die Anzeigenredaktion schließt abends um neun
die Kinosäle werden abgedunkelt, etwas mehr Leben

yellow-red fire
in a scrap yard,

gentle, gentle woods, last remains of
forests in which the thin morning fog
still hangs, traces of dampness, not

bent over, small peaceful ponds, forgotten

at the edge of an estate (:"we're coming back,"
in that house, we're coming home, home?) for the eyes
a fugitive rest, from the train window

looking out, the long, slow

even view across this country. There is a
hunkered-down green, fantastic green, which passes by,
and a child's hand stretched out the train

window.

Why sadness? All: you gentle

faces in the afternoon light (no faces
: you gentle faces between for the coins)
the billboards, you gentle

faces in the window frames,

you gentle faces in the September light, you
gentle faces of West Germany, tired and sad,
you gentle faces, hungry for cunt, cock,
tits, hungry for an exotic everyday

life, hungry for a kiss, hungry
to feel your own kiss between the walls,

hungry between the advertisements, hungry between
the classified ads, hungry between the pictures,

the advertising sales department closes at nine in the evening
the movie theaters are darkened, to show a

zu zeigen, die Kassen schließen eine
Viertelstunde nach Beginn des Hauptfilms,

die Fernsehstation sendet bis kurz nach
12 nachts, hungrig in den engen

        Gärten, hungrig nach einer sanften Umarmung,

was gebt ihr euch selbst? Was ist das für eine Art
Erschrecken, bleibt man mitten auf der Straße
stehen unter den Passanten,

                        & jeder für jeden ein Passant.

little more life, the box offices close a
quarter-hour after the main feature begins,

the television station broadcasts until shortly after
midnight, hungry in the narrow

gardens, hungry for a gentle embrace,

what do you give your selves? What kind of a
horror is that, when one stops in the middle of the street,
standing among the passers-by,

& each for everyone a passer-by.

Acknowledgments

The author gratefully acknowledges the following publications in which some of these translations originally appeared: *Atlanta Review*, *Basalt*, *Chelsea*, *Circumference*, *Denver Quarterly*, *Full Metal Poem*, *Great River Review*, *Green Integer Review*, *International Poetry Review*, *Jacket*, *Like a Pilot* (Sulphur River Literary Review Press), *Luna*, *Mantis*, *Origin*, *Partisan Review*, *Poetry International*, *Sulphur River Literary Review*, *Talisman*, *Washington Square*, *Whispering Villages: Seven German Poets* (Longhouse), Under Glass (Longhouse) and *Van Gogh's Ear*. "Some Very Popular Songs" was published as a limited edition chapbook by Toad Press.

About the Author

Rolf Dieter Brinkmann was born in Vechta, Germany, in 1940, in the midst of World War II, and died in 1975, in London, England, after being struck by a hit-and-run driver. During his lifetime, Brinkmann published nine poetry collections, four short story collections, several radio plays, and a highly acclaimed novel. He also edited and translated two important German-language anthologies of contemporary American poetry (primarily Beat and New York School, for which Brinkmann had a particular affinity), and translated Frank O'Hara's *Lunch Poems* into German, as well as a collection of poems by Ted Berrigan, entitled *Guillaume Apollinaire ist Tot*. In May, 1975, just a few weeks after his death, Brinkmann's seminal, parameter-expanding poetry collection *Westwärts 1 & 2* appeared, which was posthumously awarded the prestigious Petrarca Prize.

About the Translator

Mark Terrill shipped out of San Francisco as a merchant seaman to the Far East and beyond, studied and spent time with Paul Bowles in Tangier, Morocco, and has lived in Germany since 1984, where he's worked as a shipyard welder, road manager for rock bands, cook and postal worker. His poems, prose, memoirs, criticism and translations have appeared in over 500 literary journals and anthologies worldwide, a dozen chapbooks, several broadsides and three full-length collections, including *Kid with Gray Eyes* (Cedar Hill Books) and *Bread & Fish* (The Figures). He recently guest-edited a special German Poetry issue of the *Atlanta Review*, which includes his translations of Günter Grass, Peter Handke, Rolf Dieter Brinkmann, Nicolas Born and many others. Currently he lives on the grounds of a former shipyard near Hamburg with his wife and a large brood of cats.

Free Verse Editions

Edited by Jon Thompson

13 ways of happily by Emily Carr
A Map of Faring by Peter Riley
An Unchanging Blue: Selected Poems 1962-1975 by Rolf Dieter Brinkmann, translated by Mark Terrill
Between the Twilight and the Sky by Jennie Neighbors
Blood Orbits by Ger Killeen
Child in the Road by Cindy Savett
Current by Lisa Fishman
Divination Machine by F. Daniel Rzicznek
Physis by Nicolas Pesque, translated by Cole Swensen
Poems from above the Hill & Selected Work by Ashur Etwebi, translated by Brenda Hillman and Diallah Haidar
Puppet Wardrobe by Daniel Tiffany
Quarry by Carolyn Guinzio
remanence by Boyer Rickel
Signs Following by Ger Killeen
The Flying House by Dawn-Michelle Baude
The Prison Poems by Miguel Hernández, translated by Michael Smith
The Wash by Adam Clay
These Beautiful Limits by Thomas Lisk
Under the Quick by Molly Bendall
Verge by Morgan Lucas Schuldt
What Stillness Illuminated by Yermiyahu Ahron Taub
Winter Journey [Viaggio d'inverno] by Attilio Bertolucci, translated by Nicholas Benson

www.ingramcontent.com/pod-product-compliance
Lightning Source LLC
Chambersburg PA
CBHW031251090426
42742CB00007B/401

* 9 7 8 1 6 0 2 3 5 1 9 8 1 *